TO
ALi BONGO
ALL THE BEST
& THANKS.

Garry & ROB
X X .

Adult Child
to
Childish Adult

ELIZA FYNN

authorHOUSE®

AuthorHouse™ UK
1663 Liberty Drive
Bloomington, IN 47403 USA
www.authorhouse.co.uk
Phone: 0800.197.4150

Published by AuthorHouse 11/13/2018

ISBN: 978-1-5462-9880-9 (sc)
ISBN: 978-1-5462-9879-3 (e)

Library of Congress Control Number: 2018911723

Print information available on the last page.

Any people depicted in stock imagery provided by Getty Images are models,
and such images are being used for illustrative purposes only.
Certain stock imagery © Getty Images.

This book is printed on acid-free paper.

Because of the dynamic nature of the Internet, any web addresses or links contained in
this book may have changed since publication and may no longer be valid. The views
expressed in this work are solely those of the author and do not necessarily reflect the
views of the publisher, and the publisher hereby disclaims any responsibility for them.

INTRODUCTION

I RARELY READ anything apart from my post, news snippets, or results from a search engine....and the odd bout of proof reading of my days' written work. I can't stay with any storyline, or information past approximately two paragraphs, my mind wanders, to the point where I might as well be staring at a wall for how much reading actually goes on or not. A leaflet I did gradually read, suggested "Lack of concentration in reading" as one of the several symptoms of depression. I do suffer from depression and Complex – Post Traumatic Stress Disorder, because of being sexually abused through childhood and adolescent years by my so called dad. https://www.nhs.uk/conditions/post-traumatic-stress-disorder-ptsd/complex/.

If I had managed to become engrossed in any books, I'd possibly get distracted from my honest feelings and words towards this writing, and feel easily influenced by other author's' words. I don't want words that have been expressed from someone else's feelings. It has to be written straight from *my* stress, aching gut and complete honesty, to deliver it how it is.

I'm often writing though, either on this laptop or pen to paper. It's my stress buster. I ease my mind by writing my often, turbulent thoughts down. Sometimes they become the brunt of letters or emails that I have to write, though some of which, I have to destroy, delete or eventually dare send. It looks and feels good too, seeing my state of mind written down, because I'm still giving whoever it is, on any day, a piece of my mind. I can call anyone anything I like and I do. If a written piece of my mind has gone to a recipient, good! They clearly deserved it and it lasts longer than me giving it verbally to them, plus the likelihood of me getting my words in a muddle is strong when attempting to give verbal hell to anyone.

This writing's been going on with eagerness for the past four years. It was shoved back as a lower priority across the eighteen years prior to that, mostly due to lone parenting, working full time and still not affording a computer, and the fact that I was putting a nightmare childhood behind me where it should belong, and sometimes learning a proper childhood from watching my Daughter India growing up

I've never written a book before. This writing's a massive jot for me, but I hope this brings you into my elaborative journey. Elaborative because I'm learning that writing a book, proofing, and edit after edit, isn't something done overnight. So if I'm going to make this huge effort to tell the ugly truths of different events in my life, and the lack of justice for them, I'll go another level on the raw details, harsh words and descriptions, because once it's published, I for sure won't have any regrets about not omitting raw facts to save face, or to further protect any perpetrator's' feelings… This isn't a fantasy story. It's the truth and nothing but. If it's looking to become too disturbing to read and you choose to say 'Bye' to it, then thank you for trying to read what I lived through… If you do continue to read on, I hope you can leave it behind once you've closed the covers, or switched off your Kindle, for your peace of minds' sake.

Dotted across the past eighteen years, I've been to various Counsellors and one Psychologist for much needed help, which they all did at the time, plus the distance of time has helped a bit, however, I've not had the proper day in court. I've not received one apology from any perpetrator, yes, there are more, they've long scarpered off. Oh! Just remembered, the rapist in Kent said sorry straight after he'd finished with me.

Doors have been slammed on me, even by who I used to call family, just for being honest about what I was having counselling for, and eventually wanting justice. So, this book is saying what I wasn't allowed to say for fifty years. I'm five decades away from the brunt of sexual abuse, eighteen years away from the first attempt of this book, yet only four years away from nearly, finally getting justice.

I now, comfortably don't give a toss about other's feelings about me being a victim of sex abuse in my childhood anymore, because those who knew about the sex abuse, who disbelieved me, and those who chose to stay quiet on it, then done supportive statements in favour of my dad, the sex abuser, clearly didn't give a toss about me. In fact, I'll enjoy writing every sentence of it. I was about to say I've been too quiet for too long, but I haven't. I've been blurting out about it during many family rows, and argument-filled, failed relationships...The thing is, I was heard loud and clear but I wasn't *listened* to, helped or believed by those who could've at least reported it for me when I was a child.

The sex criminal is a manipulative being, an intimidator and a totally selfish bastard. My ones have had their moment/s of sexual satisfaction stolen from my body and they've lived the secret since. I've well and truly served my sentence of living their sex crimes. .

They'll know damn well it's them further into this read. Them, including my dad, have had their satisfaction from my body, then gone on to live with themselves, to bring up their own families, provide for them and protect them from others like themselves.

I hope all you perverts get flashbacks of your sick and selfish crimes upon me, as often as I get them. People say, when you hate someone, there's love there because you wouldn't have such strong feelings. They abused, raped and rubbished my body. When I hate these perverts, I want to kill them.

There's nothing in my mind that can find one iota of feeling for these scrapes of the devils' arsehole. So here, I'm entering my experiences, of what's probably the normal family life, like the bonds and behaviours, then, in my case, followed by the dysfunctional to disbanded stuff, which still possess my thoughts today.

There's love and adoration, mashed up with experiences of neglect and sex abuse. There are some real, genuine funny laughs during those innocent mis-behaviours as a child, paralleled with a silent, gut wrenching and confusing existence during my vital early years, then, into the later years, onto the freedom, away from the actual sex abuse, yet unavoidably, carrying memories threaded with anguish, at the mental sabotage of that past, then my approach to the judicial system.

During this mishmash of goings on, the childish antics and music has been a welcome distraction across the sixties and seventies whilst the parents were, frequently absent. Various songs and instrumentals of that era still frequently flash to mind. I can be busy at work, doing housework or writing, and without any prompt from my surroundings, flashes of a song, or instrumental, enter and exit my head like on auto-play, just as easily as flashbacks of the crimes that's gone on. Some of the music ones manage to bring a smile to my face, like when I flashback to the youngest of my brothers and I, dancing in the living room of our flat, to 'The Liquidator', and 'Israelittes' at 'Blow the bloody doors off" loud, yet, just as easily, I can hear the sounds of the parents arguing and fighting, or the voice, along with the stench of tobacco of my dad's' breath can snap to mind. and nostrils.

Sometimes, there *are* prompts from my surroundings that trigger the flashbacks. It's so easy to be working away conscientiously, and if I have my ipod or a radio on in the background, then Band of Gold, Suspicious Minds etc comes on, I'm straight off into that era, usually walking around the main flat I was sexually abused in as if I'm in the spirit world revisiting it, or I'm behind a camera filming the flat...Anyway, I've included song titles during this read, for certain scenes because they're just as much a part of my life, as the experiences themselves. One triggers the picture, or sounds and smells of the other.

I include the experience of todays' justice system, of how it helped me immensely at first, to make some kind of sense of my life, and learned that I wasn't wrong to seek justice Then, how it slammed doors on me and the impact that had on me.

Writing scathing letters to my dad, my main perpetrator and shouting about the sex abuse on and off all my life, then having the judicial system failing me, didn't only not help me, but it actually had *me* ending up with a police caution.

Me being cautioned, for sending dad, my sex abuser, stroppy letters, is one of the biggest "What the fuck??" moments I've ever experienced, seriously, I experienced profound disbelief whilst being arrested, and the rest of what went on whilst in a Wiltshire Police station, here in the UK ... But it was also the most awesome feeling, writing those stroppy letters, reading them again, and knowing my nonce dad read them too. I'm copying them into this read later.

I'm trying to set this out, to show some sort of a normal family life, then onto the sick stuff through my childhood, and the many house moves with further abusive experiences, and onwards into these days

Multiple sex abuse and rapes, happens. It happens to far too many children, and vulnerable adults of both sexes. One account of sex abuse or rape, is one too many. It seems the more abuse one suffers, the more we let it happen, maybe it's because we don't recognise the limits and when to say 'no' to prevent it, but even when we have learned to say 'no' it usually goes unheard anyway.

North London...
November 1960

SO, I STARTED off in London N5. I was born and named Eliza in our house. It was a beautiful, grand old house, from a basement to the second floor. It was once fully occupied with my somewhat loving and happy family.

I was born to two parents, two brothers, and my two Irish Grandparents, and sometimes dads' sister, my Aunt Helen was there, and a lady called Bella, who's no relation to any of us, she lived on the top floor. Just as well it's a huge house.

The brothers... The eldest is six years older than me, and the other one is five years my senior. The eldest brother was often the boss over us, he knew everything, so he claimed, and liked to make sure we knew that too. The younger one had a more humour and a detailed side towards any argument with the other one before the two often got punching the daylights out of each other...and the circles of their fights, some serious, some play fighting, continued throughout the years.

My Irish Grandparents, Jack and Caitlin were dads' parents, who owned the house. Aunt Helen, I believe was living in Dublin during these times. The Grandparents lived in the basement flat, and we had the middle two floors. It wasn't all that far from the old Arsenal Football Stadium. and the new Emirates Stadium.

I was four years old when mum, dad, brothers and I moved from North London to a flat in South London, and some years after, the grandparents also moved from there to a bungalow in coastal Essex.

1

Aunt Helen met and married an Italian man, Luigi, and had a son, they went on to a maisonette in East London and stayed there, and that was us gone from The Arsenal.

Aunt Helen was a beautiful woman, with long black hair. She had rich, clear blue eyes, thick mascara on, as always, and black, brushed eyebrows, which framed those deep-set eyes, perfectly. She had high cheek bones, straight nose, and lips perfectly balanced, and rarely without the red lippy on, stunning. I know she worked, but can't remember what she done.

I wish she'd been closer with me, and that we'd visited each other much more often, but I didn't see her since I was approximately ten years old, She might've found and brought out the feminine side of me during my teenage years …well, maybe…, instead of being the hard minded biker-woman I became. Come to think of it, she cut her ties from the rest of the family. I wonder, if she and I had kept in touch, would I have learned more that's not good about dad.

Well, now it's about my late Irish Grandad. He was a strong, solid man, stocky, with large, muscular arms. A genuine, gentleman he was, and so full of care and love. He was sensitive, kind, and clever, as a mechanical engineer.

His later years' employment up to his retirement was maintaining the mechanics of the rides at Butlins Holiday Camp. He'd fix anything that had busted and problem solve for anyone, in fact he could master any task put before him, whether mental or physical and he was not one to gloat about his abilities, he just knuckled down conscientiously until the job was done. If it was done perfectly, he was quietly satisfied with *that*, as opposed to himself for having done it.

When we went out, he often wore the polo shirts of those days and trousers with braces, a tweed style jacket and a trilby hat. He too, had deep set blue eyes. He had a stronger bridged nose, than Aunt Helen, and had a muscular jawline. I also remember the diamond patterned lines worn into his neck, and his wavy forehead lines.

A Grandad trait, was his pipe, and at Christmas, his cigars. It was fairly traditional in most households I guess, that the grandparents visit their sons, daughters and grandchildren, and the whole, cigar smoke-filled living room thing going on, clearing to the aroma of tangerines and hints of whisky fumes wafting around. It was a rich and indulgent atmosphere, which didn't happen often enough.

Grandad did eventually go onto smoking more roll ups than the pipe, and had a roll up making machine, where the rizla-paper goes into the material holder to steady it, then the tobacco, and filter tip. I used to enjoy the process of making them and seeing the perfect roll ups appear when the box was shut. I was given the job of making them up for him for the next days' work during my stays there most school summer holidays.

I used to brush the remaining hair he had, which was bald on top apart from a few longer strands going across. These short timeframes of togetherness have become the most treasured memories.

Monkey nuts…Random I know, but they gave us good teamwork and entertainment. He'd crack the shells, and I, with my smaller fingers, used to peel the inner papery skin off them. Not *all* of them ended up on the floor, I used to laugh at his expressions and some of the comments he used to crack, especially when I'd made good roll ups, or stuffed the pipe tobacco properly, or braved the sea when he took me to the beach at Jaywick. In his heavy voice and Irish accent, he'd say *"Ah by jove, she's done a beautiful roll up there she did nan"* and *"Ah b'Jesus, our Eliza's a cracker, a real beauty!"* I have to admit, we were a great team when it came to those short tasks, and then I'd beat him at five-card brag in the evenings.

There was something about him that made the daily things, which are usually quickly forgotten about, (if noticed at all), become enriched with character Seriously, the most basic of things, like when he used to slice their uncut, brown Hovis bread holding the loaf in one large hand. If the bread had already been started, he'd spread real butter on that started end, *then* he'd saw through the loaf, towards his chest with the knife in the other hand. I don't know what nan thought about him cutting it towards himself but it looked like he was careful. He used to wink and smile at me after cutting a slice off and giving it to me. Thinking of that real butter taste on the old Hovis still makes my mouth water today.

I remember nothing bad. There **was** nothing bad or threatening emanating from him or Nan. I only remember feel-good, thankfully.

I used to get tense now and again, when I was asked questions about religion, or even if they just talked about it. I also tensed up when asked why I never helped with washing up at home etc. I wasn't encouraged to get involved and learn. It wasn't the kind of environment for team effort at home, so I was oblivious to the fundamentals working around me during my infant/junior years. It's still more a feeling of good gone on with the grandparents, than I can think of ever really having with the parents.

So, now I move on to my late Irish Nan. She was approximately 5ft and petite. She was a nurse in her working years. She had a pale complexion, with black shoulder length wavy hair, tinged with grey. Her green eyes had a knowing, studious look about them. Her top lip was pointed in the middle towards the bottom lip, yet balanced, with her small chin. I remember her wearing sleeveless and short sleeved smart blouses, with handkerchiefs popped under one sleeve, she usually had a thin cardigan on top, and with these, she wore shin length skirts, some pleated all round, some kilt style. . She used to wear the same footwear as was in fashion when I started work years later, we called them granny sandals. Leather flats, usually closed heel, and small buckle at the ankle, then thin straps widening across the top of the feet, with open toes. The wider straps had holed patterns across them. She was always fresh looking and smartly dressed.

I used to sit at her dressing table and look through her rosary beads, then stare at the crucifix up on the wall with Jesus on it, and thinking, "That must hurt!".

She had one of those old perfume bottles with the squeeze ball to apply it, which I did. Nan and Aunt Helen had put their old make-up, hair grips, rollers and jewellery in an old make-up bag for me to play with. Even though I was already into football and motorbikes then, I enjoyed the colourful looks and how weird haired I became at the dressing table. Then it was Nan's turn for a hairdo. She smiled so much when I used to do her hair, even though it was quite an ordeal getting the rollers in, it was far worse getting them out again, but it was our fun. I used the eyebrow brush, and lippy extensively too, more of a clown over than make over I guess.

With that colourful fun had, and another day, a Sunday actually, dawned... ... ...

It's back to one of those tense moments, when Nan took me to Sunday school. It was something I looked forward to before actually joining it, because it was in a bungalow, again, but facing out onto the beach. I was dropped off by Nan, and she arranged to come back to get me a couple of hours later.

We were all sat down in this bungalow of religion. Some on chairs, most of us sat on the floor, and some guy was like, over there, chatting away forever. I didn't have any idea what the guy in this Sunday school was going on about. I was about five years old, and the only thing I knew about religion, was nothing actually. I just wanted something to eat and drink and play on the beach.

I was asked a question, and I thought, 'Oh no, me!' I hadn't been listening because I was bored shitless and about to nod off. I knew my eyelids were heavy, and my cheeks were red for this tiredness and boredom. I remember saying 'Jesus?', whilst glancing around hoping no one's annoyed with me. I didn't even hear the question properly, and certainly didn't understand whatever it was I did hear. I don't know what he said to Nan, but I wasn't taken back there again. Yeah, that was tense for me.

In their two (they moved to a different bungalow a couple of years later) bungalows in coastal Essex, and their trailer, on the trailer park more inland Essex, there were crucifixes in every room. Nan had her pale blue glass rosary beads, which she used to pass each bead at a time, through from one hand to the other, silently mumbling, something, I don't know. It could have been Gaelic, could've been anything, and I'm sure it gave her hope and maybe she felt better afterwards.

I often peeked at Nan engrossed in those prayers, and doing what she done with those beads. Her face was always hung in sorrow. She probably prayed for a stop to fighting etc because Nan and Grandad looked absolutely downhearted when the news was on telly, especially about the growing Northern Ireland conflict, which they vented their disgust at.

In the London and Essex home, bungalows and trailer, during their dinner preparation, I was guaranteed to be on the scene at some point, not just because I love my food, but mostly. Anyone's mouth would water at the aroma of nans' cooking. She was often, pretty fussy about the cuts of meat at the butchers, and just the same when the butcher came round the park in the van. She knew the way to grandads' heart was via his stomach alright, and she done huge, near plate size steaks, with mash, peas and thick gravy, which was a regular sumptuous mountain. I'd have a miniature version, and a slice of bread, (again yes… buttered), to wipe the plate clean.

Nans' fry ups of eggs, bacon, mushrooms and tomatoes, and Grandad had black pudding with his, unbeatable, and the liver and bacon with cabbage and mash, and that deelish thick gravy again. Every dinner cooked by Nan, was filled with full on flavour, colour, heart and soul.

They doted on me and showed their love for me in the most wholehearted possible way. I'm glad someone did.

Nan was often busy in the background, working for grandad and I, and sometimes Aunt Helen, but when we did get time together, she would tell me short stories in her quiet and oh so gentle way, often saying as a link between sentences, "*It is*" (even if it wasn't, whatever it was), I was entranced as she'd carry on in her soft voice and Irish accent into the story, or of her past.

My Grandad also told me stories, mostly in their first Essex bungalow in my bedroom while Nan got ready for bed. It was all clean and innocent, with no worries of inappropriate actions. Quite often though, during those warm nights, and with my thoughts of S London and parents flashing in and out of my head. Just as grandad settled back down in the living room with Nan, I would feel that trickle onto my cheek or lip, where one of my regular nose bleeds had started. They were so patient and calm with me about it.

I can even remember their patience with me back in N London, nearly every morning, early, when I was approximately three years old, I used to get out of bed, creep downstairs, and strip off on route to their bed, and they'd wrap their blankets round me and nan used to hug me. I never know to this age, why I stripped off…*They* had nightclothes of some sort on.

I had no thoughts of them touching me inappropriately, and I'm sure they had none of those thoughts either, because they never did touch me, apart from a loving hug. They were decent, clean and loving, a trustworthy and honest couple.

It's strange but true, they both always said that when one of them passes away, the other one would join them within three weeks, and that's exactly what happened during my teenage years. Grandad died June 1974 and Nan died July that year. How on earth did they know that? It was a brain tumour that took Grandad, and not sure what Nan died of, but it happened within the three weeks. They're both buried together in a small, beautiful cemetery in Essex. God bless you lovely two…even though I don't understand religion, I'm sure there's a god for those two xx

Now on to my late Mum, Hazel, she was five foot six, with long, dark, naturally wavy hair, which always shone deeply, as it bounced up and down her back. Her features were more like Hawaiian than English in her younger years, with her hazel eyes, lovely level white teeth, and attractive smile.

As far back as I can remember, during our years in Kent, she'd suffered from Narcolepsy, a sleeping illness, which had her falling asleep during most days and evenings on the settee. She had no control of it. It wasn't a fully recognised illness then, so she wasn't given drugs really good enough to combat it, nor was she having reviews on it. It's not a well known illness even these days. There was hardly any quality of life for her, and sadly, it was very debilitating.

It wasn't nice for us three youngsters, coming in from school or playing outside, and seeing her asleep, again. As youngsters, at first, we found it funny, but it was far from that. She couldn't come to school events like most other parents did, she couldn't drive. She had to rely on me to wake her up when we went on the bus to swimming club and coach trips to swimming galas. Poor health dogged her later life.

She was generally a more sheltered kind of woman, who rarely fought or argued back to correct dad, but when she did have energy to strop out, she really used it and gave hell.

I'm sure she suffered from depression. When we lived in Kent, she couldn't work because of the illness, and there was no socialising really, apart from the rare visit to bingo with one or two of her three sisters in the early seventies, and out to the swimming club every Friday evening in S London, then up the road to my Uncle and Aunt's' house.

Mum was very often having nightmares and waking up crying about something at least once a week, but nobody outside the house would know the dark world she existed in. I guess, with us as kids, not being brought up with hugs, or any love shown by her, explains why during those shock awakenings, of mum screaming and crying, I never thought to hug her.

She always slept on the settee at night, so when I was woken up in a start by mum wailing out loud, I had to rise rapidly out of bed and charge downstairs, bunging the light on quickly and make her a cup of tea, then ask what that one was about, (and hoping the neighbour didn't get woken up too) and she'd say what they usually were about, "Spiders", "The old cow" (mums' ex best friend Rose), or "Someone trying to break into the house"

That burglar one, used to scare me because she used to tell me to check the back door's locked, after nearly convincing me she heard someone rattle the door handle. The only luu in that house was just outside and to the left of that back door, with no outer door for years, until Irish grandad eventually visited and fitted one there.

Of course, getting up during the night, made me want the luu, and I was in complete fear of turning the key to unlock the back door, in case something creepy pushed the door into me. I'd then charge to get into the luu, and bolt that door rapidly, whilst mum locked the back door again and listened out for me to unbolt the luu door, with the whole process again, with me fearing someone's waiting outside the *luu* door, then speed back into the kitchen in spine-chilling terror and locked up.

All that fear because of that recurrent bloody nightmare. I would then see she's alright to be left alone there with the light on and a cuppa. We had no overnight telly to watch then and definitely no mobile phones to text each other on.

Mum could have good days, when she'd got up and ready for the day quickly, like for appointments, or a rare day out to Margate on the train, with myself and a friend. Other times though, Mum was exhausted before her day started, with the depression and nightmares

I don't know what her full background was, apart from some things she told me about being evacuated during the war, somewhere up north but I can't remember exactly where. Mums' dad and a brother had died in the war when she was young. She later had a stepfather, who I knew as grandad Fred, who was another intelligent man, an engineer in the RAF.

With losing a Father and Brother to the war, and later on losing a baby during the birth, I can only guess she was suffering from the equivalent of ptsd, what many people suffer from today. I suppose having lived and slept with dad in the past as well, is it any wonder she suffered from depression and nightmares?

She met dad when he was in the army, and she was working in S London, where she done a wiring and soldering job. It was a well-established work place at that time.

She just wanted stress free living, no confrontations. She was always kind and generous, to which some people took advantage, only the once though. She had smiles for anyone whilst out shopping or attending hospital appointments. It's like she was acting her life out. If there was a rare hug from her, I can't remember it one bit. She never really showed love for us three, but she was definitely a worrier about us, which I guess was her way of love for us.

Mum had three sisters, and In her fitter days, before she was married, she used to go out on pushbikes with her sisters, and ride to what's locally known as the Glory Bumps on heathland, from S London, a good 5 miles, then riding over the 'glories' for a few hours, then back. I still can't imagine her young, fit and healthy though.

Her mum, my English Nan, Olive, was tall, she also had thick wavy hair, she had large blue eyes. She always had an apron on and those funny old slippers with the bobble on top at the front. A traditional and softy old English pair, her and Grandad were. English grandad was a bit shorter than her, and of slight build, and a pale complexion, he too was baldish on top, like the Irish grandad.

During those earlier years, I remember being dropped off to their maisonette also in S London some odd afternoons, and having oxtail or tomatoe soup and chatting with the other lovely grandad when he'd finished work.

I can't remember much more about these two. I didn't see much of them at the maisonette. I remember them visiting us a couple of Christmases. All that was not to last long though, because of *more* breakdowns in family relationships meant I didn't visit them anymore. That's about all I know about mums' past. Mum died of Ischaemic Heart Disease, aged 59, in 1992.

Nonce "Dad"

NOW, IT'S ON to the dark side of the jot, 'Dad', shame I can't mention this ones' name, as much as I'd like to… and should do.

Strange how things turn out isn't it. I write about the 'late' Mum and 'late' Nans' and Grandads, and later in this read the 'late' Rose. All those people who had a little bit more time for me in the clean and healthy way. Then when it comes to the filthy bastard. It still exists.

During the early years of mine, he was 5ft 8, a bit stocky, with black hair, dead straight and Brylcreemed back, like Reg Varney from On The Buses series back in the 70's, but the long fringe would still fall over his face. He had no health problems I was ever aware of. He used to have clear, brilliant blue eyes, and dimples in his cheeks. He had a tattoo marking his service in the army in Hong Kong. He had some other tattoos, but he didn't have us three kids' names done. Maybe we've always been an embarrassment to him.

When we lived in N London, he was a bus driver. Dad later became a railway worker down at the nearby S London rail station when we moved to the flats, where from the flat, he also ran the Tenants' Association for the housing estate during the 1960's. He had other employment, but hey.

I remember him often working on the old cars in N London, and outside the flats we lived in after there. I only remember going out a couple of times with him, and even they created horrendous memories.

Dad always lectured me and the brothers on manners, and made himself believe how great, impressionable and almighty he was, and us, in return, had to act like some sort of ambassadors for this often, dirty, grease covered, boiler suited, body odorous greb.

He insulted us in front of anyone if it gained him attention, and it was usually some unimpressed woman with a short skirt on.

In N London, when I was about three years old, dad and I walked down to the Arsenal tube station. I remember, when on the platform, the echoing sounds going on for ages, of the last train gone through, and the draft from the black arched tunnel, as the train bored through our history of dust.

He picked me up, counted to three as he swung me back and forth, then let go of me for an instant, then he grabbed me in mid-flight after making me believe he was really chucking me onto the rails. I remember screaming N5 down, because I was picturing me going into that frightening blackness or being hit by the next train, which was on its way, yet I still put my trust in him to not throw me again, as I fell for it a couple more times that we went there.

It's hard to keep referring to him as 'Dad'. He has never properly been there for us three as youngsters, or throughout the rest of my childhood from about 1965. It's not as if he wasn't there for us because he was in active service, because he had long before, left the army. I also can't refer to him as 'Dad', because of the events, that happened during and since the 1960's, proves he has no right to be given the title of dad or any kind of father figure nickname. He just was not there for us three.

He's now known as 'shitface' by me. It's the easiest sound to make when he flashes to mind. This may seem harsh, (unless you've lived with the guy), but repetitions of 'cunt' won't get this published.

I was writing, his name as 'shitface' throughout, but not only did it become boring to write and proof read, but writing 'shitface' doesn't clarify the reality of stuff gone on, for example. "I held onto shitface's' penis, can be general sex between two stroppy adults...whereas, "I held onto dads' penis", reveals the sick truth of what it was...and words that shouldn't ideally be in the same sentence.

So, We Know Who's Who In The 'Family', Now Let's Get To Know More.

I GUESS INITIALLY it was the typical run of the mill family life for me. It's clear I was pretty spoilt by the grandparents, and had a loving bond with them, unlike I had with the parents.

I was chubby, I mean v-e-r-y chubby. I was a fat, dimple cheeked, gypsy looking girl with waist length hair, which was plaited down my back. I started to be a tomboy at that early age.

The first things I remember playing, were, 'snail races', in the back garden in N London. I used to line a few snails up on the low wall in the long back garden, and give them a bit of time to get slithering along. When I decided there's a winner, I would pick it up and paint its shell. The paintbrush with a dab of paint on supplied by Grandad of course. It came out better than the loser, which I used to get excited about, before stamping on it. No one explained to me how cruel that was. I guess my Irish Nan prayed for forgiveness for me in her morning, noon and nightly prayers.

Nan, Grandad, and Aunt Helen lived by the Catholic religion, so I'm sure one of them would've sought help for me in their prayers at different times... If only they knew about the sex abuse!

Another 'game' I played, lasted all of once. Still in N London, Grandad had built a huge framework, from rough wood, which I kept trying to climb, but for each time I attempted it, I was told off by Mum & Nan

As soon as they were busy chatting again, I charged from the back door, halfway up the garden to the framework, and sprung up onto the angled, support timbers, and immediately understood why I was being stopped from climbing it, with the rest of the day spent digging and plucking huge splinters out from head to toe.

I tell myself these are normal childhood happening's, I guess it was during the sixties, if that's what you call normal. Some childhoods were better, some I've learned since, were far worse.

When I was two or three, I was the first one out of bed one morning and was determined to cook the parents a breakfast whilst they were still in bed. I was trying to be like Nan. However, the ever bossy, eldest brother was blocking me from putting the cooker on, and my other brother joined in, trying to stop me. The arguing was getting louder.

During our fight, I'd been turning the dials, trying to get the flames to show. There was a cease fire for a minute or two, because the brothers were distracted, explaining to the parents, what the "bloody hell's going on".

There was a false wall behind the cooker, which I hid behind after turning a few more dials. It wasn't very long before I got caught in my hiding place, and our fight resumed.

They tugged at me and shouted. I wailed back at them, whilst attempting to win this tug of brothers v fat girl war, I leant back, whilst skidding and juddering my fat little feet as they squeaked along the floor, and by now bawling my eyes out, I broke free and pressed, turned something or lit a match? can't remember, but ignited the cooker, and flash!

Within seconds of the explosion, I was scrambling up off the floor from the wall opposite, less my fringe, eyebrows and lashes, and with the awful smell of singed hair, which stayed for days, possibly weeks.

It seemed like all the occupants were shouting, when my bolshie dad stormed onto the scene, roaring my first lecture at me, and gave me a heavy clout on the hand. ...Well that's the last time I attempt to cook breakfast for them.

Well I can only guess this was a typical run of the mill family life, because it's normal in comparison to the following years.

Obviously, at the age of about two or three, we wouldn't usually have done things, which created life time memories, unless it's significant. Yeah, like the cooker incident.

My earliest recall of sex abuse incidents was when I was two or three years old.

It comes to me when *it* decides to kick off in my head, and anything can trigger it, like the smells of nicotine, body odour, or even if someone speaks in a tone like mum did at this first incident.

There was mum sat on a chair, with her left breast out, I'd been put on her lap. Dad was crouched down to my right, telling me to put my mouth on her nipple, or whatever he called it, I can't remember the words, probably because the actions were speaking louder. I was going shy, and smiley, whilst covering my face with my arm, saying, and nodding "No". I simply didn't want to do that!

It was lovely sitting on Mums' lap. If only it was just for love or hugs, sadly not. I remember Mum saying "Ohw no M*****, stop it!". He must've forced her to get her breast out. He was very fidgety and breathing erratically, whilst saying in a panic "Go on!"

I said 'no' several more times because I felt uncomfortable and shy, and by this time, about to cry at thoughts of doing that, but my face was pushed onto her breast by him. I can only assume now, (going on our history) that he was bringing himself off...sexually satisfying himself, masturbating, wanking himself off, .whatever language you use for this. He wasn't taking photographs, or doing a portrait drawing, whilst doing what I was forced to do,

I don't know why mum didn't fight and protect me from him forcing me to do that. I don't know where anyone else was at the time. I can't change what happened. I tried to choose not to do that, but my choice was overridden by the strength of him and his selfishness.

That was my earliest memory of dad using me for his sexual satisfaction, even though I didn't actually see him giving himself a hand job, all the movements, shaken breathing, and desperation in his voice, matched the scenes and sounds of his actions during following incidents.

It was strange because even then, I didn't get hugged by them, yet being allowed to sit on mums' lap was lovely, but it wasn't for a hug, or any kind of closeness. It was for him.

The Flats South London 64/65 Until 69/70.

Darkly To Dad And Back

THIS WAS OUR decent sized, first floor, three bedroomed flat. It has a lounge diner, with a hatch from the diner end, to the kitchen, and has a bathroom separate from the toilet.

With the presence of Mum sometimes dad included, it had beautiful plants colouring all of the balcony and living room, and the aroma of dinners, more often than not something & chips.

Without the presence of Mum... and rarely with dad either... Dead plants in dried out, shrunken soil, and three of the rooms became crime scenes, and quite nice dinners at Rose's' flat across the green and to the left of our flat.

Songs that flash to mind and of these flats are, 'Those Were The Days by Mary Hopkin. Downtown by Petula Clark, The Mighty Quinn by Manfred Mann, Blackberry Way by The Move. Israelites by Desmond Dekker and The Aces and The Liquidator by Harry J and The All Stars. There are other songs, like Captain of Your Ship, and White Horses etc, which take me back to these days, but the flashes of the flat, and the crimes within, appear from hearing these ones.

I was four years of age, when Mum, dad, brothers and I moved to this flat. Mum had a close friend called Rose, who lived in the long block of flats, which ran alongside ours and another block opposite.

Rose was on the second floor and we could see her flat from our first floor one. She had 3 sons, the eldest was a couple of years older than my oldest brother, and the middle and youngest were of similar age to them. Rose's husband was always away, in the Royal Navy

When I was about five years of age, mum had left us. I had no idea why, or whether it was forever or temporary. In hindsight, I think she had a breakdown since going full term in pregnancy, because during the birth, the cord went around the babys' neck and my newbie sister was gone.

She was going to be called 'Kimberly' or 'Kim'

I had been feeling jealous, yet quite excited about having a new baby in the flat. Dad, during all of this going on, was going over 'Rose's' flat probably every spare moment he had.

One evening, they (dad and Rose) came over to our flat, which was a rarity for her, she entered my bedroom, she broke the news to me about the baby. Dad told the brothers in their bedroom. I was naturally gutted, because I was waiting to see what she looked like, and hold her. I was confused about why dad, or mum where ever she was, didn't tell me, and why Rose told me.

Nobody talked about Mum to me, apart from being told she has gone away for a while. I remember visiting her in hospital one day, and feeling gutted about leaving her there, but that could've been another reason what she was in hospital for.

It wasn't the same at home without mum there, whether she loved me or not, it still choked me.

Most of my infant school days didn't seem to be happening. I did attend them alright, but my thoughts were pre-occupied with wondering if I will ever see my mum again...Was she dead and no one is telling me? Doesn't she like me? Why doesn't she like me?

Then my thoughts turned to the stuff I was doing with dad most evenings. "His willy was big and straight". "It was wet, horrible and sticky". "He really likes me when it's 'our secret time'". "I don't want to do that again". Then thoughts of, could it all be because I still spoke with dad, why mum won't come home to see me? I often thought this too because there were many rows between them dotted across the months or years.

17

By the time my thoughts had gone over and over the same questions and visions, I had missed most of what was being taught during class time.

I had to sneak a peek at someone's' story in class. Frances was sat next to me, she went to the luu. I got caught copying her work, and told off for not listening. I just accepted the telling off.

Walking to and from school was a blur because of wondering if/ when mum's coming back home, and where has she gone?

It's not fair, everyone else has their mum or brothers and sisters with them. My brothers go to the senior school together, and I had to walk to Normandy school without Mum or dad.

The main road alongside the school was always busy, I had to cross it to get to school and back home. A lovely lad, a school friend of mine was killed on that road when he was six years old. Further up that road, another friend of mine was hit by a car after school. You really had to run for your life most schooldays trying to get across it, yet somehow, I got there and back ok by myself, even though mentally, I was miles away.

Just because the weekends arrived, it didn't mean things were safer and better… It was just another set of shite scenarios. Dad had to tend to my Sunday bath times, seeing as mum wasn't there.

Each bath time started off fine, and I guess no different from any other childs' bath time.

I'd have my bottle of bubble bath, which was in the shape of a poodle dog, with its front legs up in the 'beg' position. It was made of clear plastic, with a groove in the plastic lid to press through, to become a money box after it's finished with. The lather had a scent like Infa-care baby bubble bath, only sweeter.

I'd enjoyed seeing the sparkle of the bubbles reflecting from the light, and picking up the lather in my hands for a closer look. I would be in the bath for a short while, then dad came in, and crouched down, and he'd say "D'ye want to play daddys' little game?" I'd nodded 'No' a few times, knowing what his game was, but it didn't make any difference, "It won't take long" he'd say.

He would shut and lock the bathroom door, then turn the light off. Then he'd talk in a childish manner to level with my young age, quietly saying "Put ye arms and shoulders forward like 'dis' to make titties" I had to make some form of a breast cleavage by moving my shoulders and arms forward.

With me being so fat, I guess it looked a bit like a bust. He said "Hold 'dis' for daddy. I had to hold dad's' erect penis. He said "hold it tight and rub it up and down like 'dis'. Dad had put my hand on his penis, with his hand on top of mine, to teach me how tight to squeeze it, and how to rub it up and down, to give him a hand job for his sexual relief. He made me take over, and carry on until he ejaculated. Dad's' semen was wiped from my hand, arm and chest, or make- believe breasts, with my flannel or sponge, can't really remember what he used, dunked in the water and then my bath was done.

One bath time, with the usual routine of the door locked and light off when he's entered. He said "D'ye want to play another game with daddy?" I smiled and said "yeah", I thought of something outside the bathroom, a proper game. He said "D'ye want to put 'dis in your mouth for daddy?"

As no surprise, he had his erect penis out again. "No", I immediately said and nodded no. "Don't ye want to try it for daddy then?", "It's alright because Mammys' and daddies play this, and it's alright for Eliza to do it for daddy", he said, whilst he was waiting with his knob, right next to my mouth. I said "No" a bit more definite and louder. Dad quickly put my hand on his penis to masturbate him until he ejaculated again.

Then he'd say "This is daddys' and Elizas' secret. That means you don't tell anyone, not even ye mammy or your brothers". So I had to nod yes, to convince this dirty old man I wouldn't tell anyone.

This is when I get really angry, reliving this shit! But if I don't write the raw details, no one gets the real picture. They just don't get it, then they make some chance, stupid remarks like "Ohw move on, don't let him rule your life". Fuck, the fuck, off! Take that void head off this planet! If I could *choose* to move on, I would've done! I don't choose to have these images, smells and sounds to gate crash my mind, they turn up!

During one bath time while dad was with me, this was a normal routine by then, he'd put the light off as usual, and the door's locked, and after a short while, I was doing what he usually made me do to him, giving that wanker a wank!...Just saying it how it was, in this angry

19

state. There was a loud knocking on the bathroom door. Dad asked "Who's that?".

The youngest of my two brothers, said, "What's going on in there!? And why's the light off!?". Dad put his penis back into his trousers and opened the door, then said whatever excuse he made, which didn't faze me because I wasn't doing anything wrong in dads' eyes.

My brother never questioned me about what was going on in the bathroom with the light off, but I did tell him in later years…and nothing was done about it. Surprise, surprise.

I was made to feel well-favoured and important by dad, in this strange sort of way, and by now, dad and I had our routine of sexual activity going on. whilst I also was thinking about the money, sweets and toys I'd be getting for being daddys' girl. I didn't get those treats, but all the big secret goings on was a sort of awesome, in its sick sort of way.

Some night times, I'd sleep in dad and mum's bed with him.

The dribble stained pillows stunk of stale dribble and nicotine. So too did dads' breath.

The bedside cabinets had an ashtray each, which had black bakelite or plastic base, sloping up in vertical panels, with silver coloured metal tops. They looked and smelt like they'd not been cleaned out since they got them.

I'd be sleeping to his left, and I'd lay on my right side, and rest my left arm upon dads' waist or hip. He'd say, "Ah is it dis you want?". Dad would turn towards me and put my hand on his erect penis, and make me do the full sexual relief on him…often.

Those smells, along with dad's' strong body odour from under his arms, and his own smell risen up the bed from his groin, and of the warm semen all over my hands, wiped off with a spat on, nicotine stained, dirty handkerchief, never made me think it was wrong, dirty or guilty towards my mum, because it was with 'dad', and I didn't know that those smells and what we were doing was dirty or wrong, because I was inside this experience, living and learning it…

I wasn't comfortable about it one bit, but telling him to 'fuck off', or calling the police, (with no phone anyway) or telling a teacher would've been the 'wrong' thing to do because it's about 'dad', and besides, I was five or six years old, and would've got a good hiding if I swore at him or told anyone, but hey ho, giving dad a hand job most nights was allowed!

Some nights, I'd be in my bed after bath time with wanker. If I got up for the toilet, then decided I wanted to sleep in his and mums' bed after, I'd go into mum and dads' bedroom, and realise he wasn't in there, or in the living room. I could hear my brothers' sleeping and breathing etc, and sadly, still no sign of mum either. He was either at work or Roses flat.

On some 'parents at home' days, my brothers were often fighting with each other, and every now and again, they'd have wrestling matches with dad, usually across the settee back, and leading to the floor by the balcony door. It did look a laugh. They'd never let me join in, no matter how many times I'd asked. It looked like fun when he wrestled with my brothers. Sometimes though, when the brothers were at Boys Brigade, or playing football, I'd ask again to play wrestling, though never holding out much hope on it.

One day, with mum still not home, I asked about it again, and was actually allowed to wrestle or pretend fight with dad.

We'd got on the settee, and dad sat opposite me and we were about to start.

Dad had button through dark trousers on with no pants underneath. I noticed, or rather, dad had made me notice his erect penis and his knob, which was red and wet.

The buttons of dad's' trousers were undone. I asked what it was. Thinking back, this must've been the start of the regular abuse. Dad was breathing erratically, then got his penis out, and said "This is daddys' (I can't remember what *he* called it), and when daddy & ye mammy want a baby, he puts it in ye mammy there like this. Somehow, I was laid down with my neck on the arm of the settee. Dad was on top of me, my head was level with his chest area, but he wasn't pressing on my body.

Dad pushed his erect penis, hard into my vagina. When he stopped, dad had ejaculated into and against my vagina. A minute or however long afterwards, he said "Did ye like daddys' and Elizas' little game?"

I don't remember answering any specific words, but it felt like 'No'.

I remember thinking "That wasn't wrestling", and "I didn't like what it was". Then "It bloody hurts".

From this wrestling/rape incident, I get images flashing of myself, and then flashes of us two, peeling my semen-soaked knickers off of my sore, reddened, wet and swollen vagina. They still happen when I remember this incident.

I was nodding to agree it's 'our secret', yet not really understanding why it was a secret, and I was deep in thought about what the hell just happened. I asked "Will I have a baby!?" Whatever he said meant no obviously. And, this was our wrestling match.

During the police investigation, my Investigating Officer mentioned briefly what dad had said about him explaining about his penis. To be brutally honest, i'd forgotten about this for several years, until she told me, then it was flashing back as I was telling her.

I don't know whether it was through my underwear, or pulled my knickers across my vagina. I'll never know…That gutless lying bastard wouldn't admit it would he! I remember it badly hurt and I was feeling claustrophobic with dad over the top of me when I couldn't move away, because he was between my legs.

I'm rolling out my vehement anger now, and imagining myself belting dad round the head with a baseball bat at his 'vulnerable' age. Letting him be controlled and hurt by me now! See how he likes it!

HELL HATH NO FURY LIKE A SEX ABUSE SURVIVOR WITHOUT JUSTICE…OR REVENGE!

THERE ARE STILL images, which flash, of dad stroking his fingers along my vagina, from the back, and up the front of it, whilst making a trumpet sound with his tightly thinned lips. He often did that when others were out of the flat, whilst i'd be getting ready for my bath or dressed for school.

There was another incident on the settee, where it may well have started off as a wrestling match, or tickling game, then dad started blowing raspberries on my legs, which was making me laugh, but being forced to wear dresses, meant dad had easy reach of my thighs and groin.

Dad continued blowing raspberries and started moving up my leg, and towards the inside leg, which led to him blowing the raspberries against my groin, and in no time atall, dad pulled my knickers across to one side of my vagina, and was continuing to blow raspberries on my groin, but licking my vagina within this game, the disgusting bastard, with all that nicotine in dad's' breath and saliva, and putting it on me.

Dad's' trousers were wet, where he'd ejaculated, so too were my knickers, vagina and groin, wet from dad's' nicotiney saliva. That disgusting, perverted paedo incident erupted as a real bad resurfaced memory during a nightmare, when my India was 6 years old.

At some point, in the days of the sex with dad, Mum had suddenly come back. I didn't know whether it was forever or not. Things were a bit more orderly, as much as they could be for this family. Suddenly, I was sleeping in my bed, and having a bath by myself, and my school uniform was ironed and aired, to put fresh on, from the clotheshorse in front of the fire if it was a chilly morning.

Some evenings, during this abuse calmed down time, if I was very lucky, I could have a cider lolly or an oyster ice cream off Papas' Ice cream van. My dresses were not cutting me in half at the belt. I had nothing to recently remember as a secret. I knew where mum was, she was at the flat.

But it's very different now I'm shell shocked and my guts are tightening daily, for mum and dad arguing and fighting nearly all the time, and my brothers are more often fighting for real, there's no wrestling match games anymore, they're all real fights.

My head's in chaos for other reasons now. Mum's agreed with Iris, the neighbour downstairs, if dad tries getting into our flat, Mum's to lock herself out on the balcony and bang the ground with the hammer, (No phones) then 'Mick', Iris's' husband, will help get dad out of the way, and it all went to plan. It actually happened. Dad entered the flat, mum banging the hammer on the balcony floor whilst shouting out to Iris. Then Mick and someone else scuffled with dad in our hallway and got dad out of the flat. I was left in the living room, to see all that, whilst Mum locked herself out. Later, I had to play in Iris jnrs' bedroom downstairs for safety from the aggressive goings on in our flat, and while Mum sorted stuff out with Iris senior. My head ached with confusion.

What the fuck is happenin'!?

ROSE…ROSE WAS WHAT the fuck's happening! I didn't understand for ages why mum was close with her for some time, and best of friends, then she's not living with us, and dad was close with Rose, and we had to have our tea there at Roses flat etc.

I remember mum being with us three in our flat, and looking out from behind the curtain across to Roses flat. She was waiting for dad to sneak out of there, and he only did. Suddenly, all hell let loose.

Mum was seriously fast, and stropping right out, "Gunna give that fuckin' ol' cow a bleedin' good 'idin!'", and all sorts of anger in motion on the way down our staircase, and marching straight out of our block across to Roses. Me and the brothers followed her as far as we could, which was into Roses block, up the stairwell to the two stairs bit on the second floor, just in sight of Roses door. I don't know where dad went. Maybe he was off down the road the opposite way to work on the night shift, and had slept at Roses that day, and Mum sussed it out, hence the spying session.

Well, the brass door knockers we all had, used to echo up and down the stairwells from a normal knock. We heard mum banging on the door…South London heard mum banging on the door! Mum was shouting as soon as the door opened, and a physical punch-up begun between them, Rose was actually screeching. Rose always had a load of curlers in, with a silky headscarf over them, but not for long on this leary day. They went flying all over the place. I had to run down the stairs and get out of the way, it scared me. I still didn't fully understand what was going on though.

In later years, it became clear to me… I wasn't the only one other than mum, giving my dad sexual relief.

I can't remember whether this was before or after the Hazel/Rose fight… Before Mum left us yet again, dad had her pinned against the bathroom wall, recessed from the hallway. Her dress was ravelled up but he had his hand against her throat, I'd wondered if he'd raped her, or, those days wondered if he'd touched her like he did to me, or had been trying to. She was shouting "Get off me!" I yelled out "Stop it!" because he appeared to be hurting her. My head couldn't contain anymore, and that sight was mental chaos! Then he said to Mum "Well go on then, tell them, tell the kids you're gunna fuckin' leave them!"

The youngest of my brothers had turned up in the hallway by now. Mums' dress was down by this point. She said "I'm going away for a while". I said, "I'll go with you mum", she replied "No Eliza, you can't come with me".

During the next awestruck moment, having suddenly learned mum doesn't want me anymore, I turned away from them, whilst their fight went far into my background and silencing down.

I walked down the rest of the hallway, staring at 'stuff', stuff that I couldn't actually see because of past visions of this flat, again, empty of mum, and all the unlawful and disgusting acts that I'd been put through from dad... Enter my first experience of billions of flashbacks...Enter my Complex PTSD

Into the living room, I weakly entered and stopped to face the balcony to my left, and now failing to choke back my tears, with the rawest of gut aches at knowing she don't want me. Mum was gone again.

I still can't remember her actually going. I used to worry deeply about mum being out through the night times, struggling against all the horrors of the night that dad told me about.

Even though mum didn't want me, I would still love her, or need her. I can't to this day decide which feeling it was.

With mum gone again, and me still going to school in a daze, I remember going into the playground in my school, I walked up to a playground supervisor on morning duty and asked her "Do you know where my Mum is?" She told me 'No'. It was as blunt as that. It seemed like every hour that passed, every time I communicated, the outcome became worse, adding to the pain.

Screaming through my mind was "I want mum!" "Where is she!?" "I have to stay with him! and the secret stuff!" "and no mum!" "School's horrid without mum walking me there and meeting me, and dad's scaring me now he's like this!" I instantaneously ached from my stomach to my head.

During this living nightmare, I was always having nose bleeds.

Most wake ups for me now, were filled with confusion and dread. Or confusion, dread and blood. It was a rooted, deep down sadness, a sheer hatred of what's going on, and stifled, for I couldn't escape it. I just didn't know what to expect, very rarely was anything nice, and even though kids can be resilient, I remember the stress I felt, I would feel stressed with worry, for mum, and about the secrets of bed times and bath times I didn't want, but had to have with dad.

When this hurt started, I became overheated, then heady and cloudy, then that tickle on my upper lip, of blood, not dripping, more of a trickle, from both nostrils.

It was probably the only attention I got, in any caring sort of way, dad, ordering me to "Pinch the bridge of ye nose" and "Hold ye head back!" Maybe he cared more about preventing blood splattering all over my clothes.

After the last few minutes of blood run, there was calmness, cooled around me and I felt peace.

It felt like I had a pale blue aura evolving around me. It was likened to the winding down from crying, to sleeping. I was bloody exhausted.

What may have been months later, I was walking home from school. Yes, still on my own because there seemingly wasn't any perverts on the streets those days… he was in my flat. I was often daydreaming about mum, and having a pang in my gut and on the brink of tears at any time of any day.

I was approaching the access road in front of our block of flats, when I noticed mum out the front. She was chatting to another neighbour with her back to me. I was absolutely made up for seeing her again.

There was a flash of confusion about why she didn't meet me from school, and an instant hope she's staying for good, but this day of pangs in the gut for her was now history. Hoping mum does like me and *is* happy to see me, I was *the* most excited kid of the sixties in that moment.

Mum was on the grassed side of the kerb opposite the front of our block. I actually didn't know what to say to her. I know I had a beaming smile as I approached her left side, and looked up to her, then in a raised voice, I said an awkwardly happy "Hello!"   It's not Mum.

The only way I can describe the next feeling was, all my thoughts crashed into a rotten shock, and utter confusion of it not being mums' face as I looked up to her. Then "Where is she!" flashed to thought, and every movement and sound froze then moved in slow motion. "Stop this horrible stuff happening to me!" was all I could think.

From that beaming smile, to a quivering bottom lip, dropped jaw, instant throat ache and wide, welled up eyes as I about turned quickly, and ran up to our flat.

Dad was out on our balcony witnessing all that. I'd taken no notice of him apart from my big smile when I thought I was walking up to mum. I thought he was on the balcony *because* of her being there and they're friends again. He had nothing to say that I can remember. I cried a little then went back to going with the flow of my crappy little life.

That was one of, or *the* most dreadful moment. I didn't want to be here anymore, yet couldn't do anything about it, because I knew nothing about death, or making myself die. I had to keep being with dad, missing Mum, walking myself to school, where I think of mum, then dad, bathroom and bed. Desperately sick of now!

The thought of running off, was way too frightening because of dads' tales of the wailing banshee that's down the bottom of our road every night, and if I ran off to the other direction, I'd be faced with the headless horseman up Avenue Road. I was trapped...or cursed. I believed that shit then.

If I'd known there was such a thing as suicide then, I would've found a way and done it, because there was nothing going on except hurt, dread and confusion every day, oh, and blood.

Another very upsetting time during this already living nightmare, was when I went to find mum.

Something or someone made me believe she was at my aunt's house, about half a mile from the flat. I wandered round there to their road. Dad must have been over Roses flat, or at work still.

I knocked on my aunts' door, she answered "Is my mum there?" I asked. "No she isn't!", she snapped, with a stern look, and giving me attitude, as if *I'd* done something wrong. I was six for fucks' sake!

She told me to go back home. I felt the throat ache, whilst my jaw dropped. I nearly cried again and started to walk away.

Someone called out "Eliza!" I looked back at their house, it was mum. It really was this time.

She asked in a panic "Does the ol' man know you're here and does he know *I'm* here? I told her no, as I'd walked back to the door, where mums' body language clarified to me I was not welcome.

She was looking down at me from the doorway, and pulled the door halfway to her back. The aunt had gone back inside.

She asked me how I knew she was there. I couldn't remember how I knew, or why I thought she was there. Mum was saying something about me going back home.

No! I couldn't stand hearing that. "Don't say that mum, tell me I can stay here with you!" was all I could think, and attempt to say.

I looked behind her, no one was there, I stretched up towards her face and pleaded with her, whispering to her face, "Mum can't I stay here too? *Please* mum?" pleading, in desperation "No you can't! because the ol' man don't know I'm here". She snapped, just like my aunt done.

It was like I was floating. I was finally becoming a mentally wrecked infant, in my state of confusion at my aunts' and mums' attitudes, then the shock that I found mum, and in no time at all, she was out of the door and walking me halfway back home, to all that stuff with dad, and double shock because mum *still* doesn't want me. It was like heartache twice within a few minutes.

She walked me halfway to the junction leading to our road, and told me to go back to the flat.

"But I don't wanna go back there, I wanna stay with you mum!" I attempted to say in my infant, gut wrenching sob. "Well you can't, and don't let him see you coming from here" she said.

I walked the last couple of roads, breaking my heart, and wishing again that I wasn't there atall. Well, if there was ever any bond between us, I think she broke it whilst giving me my marching orders in that moment

Mum should've really missed me, and allowed me to stay with her. She shouldn't have left me in the first place. Mum showed no signs of want or hope for me whatsoever...It was basically "Go, don't come back".

(Later years did see my Aunt and I getting along fine).

Time Out

THROUGHOUT THAT NEAR miserable existence, there were some quiet moments, and sunny days, when I was out playing, usually on my own though. I often used to pick a particular weed, and hold it in my hands for ages, sniffing it frequently, and feeling much calmer. It's not like being stoned, (which only gave me migraines when tried it many years ago). It's more a sedate calm.

This weed was often growing between the paving slabs, and on the dried, muddy edges of the fields and kerbs around these flats. It's still something I do now. It's now called 'Pineapple weed' because it's said the leaves smell like pineapples, but I think it smells like a sweeter, fresher Chamomile, and looks similar to it.

Just sniffing its' sweetness nowdays takes me back to sitting on the hot paving slabs in our road.

There I am. It's a balmy 1960's sunny day. I see only myself, sat cross legged, with my red shorts on, my multi-coloured, horizontal striped sloppy joe, and my beige sandals. I'm sniffing the same wild-weed as I do today. There are Dandelion clocks floating around, and more butterflies, than we ever see these days, flickering across the wasteland over the road from me. I also see me walking through this wasteland, which I often did in warm weather. It's full of rubbish, which the weeds and wild flowers hid in summer times, as they were easily my chest height. Back with me on the hot pavement, I see my thick, soft hair shining. It's a vacuum of silence. There's no mum or dad around me, or sounds of arguing, or thoughts of our sex. It's just one, very, still, very silent moment, of a sweet scent, sun high, a bright blue sky, warmth and innocence, caught in a flash of my memory… .aaand gone, just like a burst bubble…and yes, I sometimes take this scented weed to bed with me during my rocky hours. I'm coming to terms that it's better than the hose to the car exhaust.

Another, childlike, childhood memory, I state with freedom and pleasure, was when I was dancing with the youngest one of my brothers to 'The Liquidator', with our hands on our hips, standing opposite each other, rocking forward and back diagonally to our shoulders. I wish I had a pound for every time we played that song. It's now on my Ipod. These memories are good snippets amongst those traumatic days.

So, the dust was kind of settling, we're getting along with the routines of the same shit another day and without mum. In our flat, after having tea in Roses' flat, I used to do anything from French finger knitting to cutting dolls' hair down to the tufts, or playing with my dolls' house etc

If my brothers were home, and not punching the daylights out of each other, we'd usually be up to some sort of funny mischief, like going into the drying-airing room just off the communal staircase, and try a puff on their once hidden cigarettes. Or going out on the roof of the communal doorway, via the first floor staircase window, which didn't used to be blocked off. One of us would be up there and try to catch a football, kicked up by the others down on the ground outside.

On another absent parent's day, I was the only one on the ground, facing an elderly couples' flat on the ground floor, about to kick the ball sideways up to my youngest brother on that roof. I had a good strong kick on me, but not the best angle, as it went powerfully through their bedroom window.

I ran up the staircase, meeting my brother scrambling back through the window, one hysterically funny site, grinning, with a giggle, then frowning and trying to run on the energy of fear, whilst barging in to each other on the landing, and through our front door.

I kind of remember being at the couples' front door apologising for breaking their window, but can't remember anyone telling me to, or what happened after.

Another misguided and funny childhood event was getting a reel of cotton from mums' sewing machine box. Me and the youngest brother, sneaking to the other five door knockers in our block, tying the cotton round and leaving it loose, unravelling the reel and fed it through our letter box, then tug it hard, hearing all or a couple of them knock... How we kept our laughs quiet I don't know.

I needed these funny little moments.

One non-school morning, still no mum around, or dad, I found it side-splittingly funny, the time both brothers stripped the beds, and tied sheets together, then hung them outside their bedroom window at the back of the flat, we abseiled down them still in our pyjamas. 'Then we ran round to the front of the block, upstairs, where the brother who didn't abseil that time, let us in'. It had me in hysterics. A neighbour must've grassed us up because dad left Rose's flat or bed, and suddenly bolted through our front door and gave us a severe and loud rollicking.

I was still in bits, laughing, and blasting snot bubbles out of my nose, tears streaming, the works, throughout his orderly lecture, I tried to pull some sort of serious face, but couldn't for now laughing at dads' anger, then at the sight of my brothers' faces.

It's been refreshing to re-live those proper childish moments. Like nothing is wrong, and all is right or funny with the world.

It's only when the appearance of dad flashes into those proper childish moments, that I also relive some of the sex abuse, which was ongoing in the bath, his bed, living room etc. I can't keep the funny stuff separate from the abuse. I try to but it arrives whatever I think. I get the visual flashes, and even the feelings of the cloudy head and an expected nose bleed, when he arrives in my head, and sometimes, a small pang in the guts if it's mum flashed up too.

Roses' Flat South London 65/66 Until 69/70

Mums' 'Best Friend'

THIS FLAT IS the longest one, which runs across the sides of all the shorter flats, and Roses flat was in view of ours. Whilst Mum was away, dad would be over her flat nearly all the time.

Rose was very house proud. Roses flat was gleaming. There was nothing out of place, ever. Everything that could shine or reflect, did so, deeply.

Mum was mostly organised and tidy to a certain level, like dust free ornaments on the gay boxes and clean, dust free shelf unit, with the large coloured brandy glasses and football trophies won by dad. Things like the washing up was done, but reluctantly later, but us three kids should've been more helpful, instead of leaving it all to mum, or maybe better still, dad could've taken his penis out of Rose and been at our flat helping mum.

Rose, house proud Rose, had a mirrored display case along the wall in the dining end of her living room, with a beautiful collection of dolls of different countries, in their traditional costumes. Not one of them was out of place, nor was there a speck of dust on the case.

There was a two tile width margin of the old fashioned black tiles round the edge of the living room carpet, and dining end, which she used to polish to the deep shine and reflections. Everything that had a surface was gleaming. She cooked lovely roast dinners and rice puddings. She was tall, upright and well kempt. She was good looking, clean and clearly spoken. There wasn't much, if anything bad about her, apart from, she wasn't mum, and she was shagging my dad. . I almost accepted them two as being very close, well I had no choice did I.

He would often stroke her backside, saying "Cor, look at dat!", and kissing it, ew, thankfully with her mini skirt *on*. I had to go over there after school for tea each evening, then home to play, then bed… to play again, with dad. We had a routine going on.

Come to think of it…If my mum wasn't sexually satisfying dad, and he goes off with her best friend… was *she* sexually satisfying him? Or is he just a plain old paedophile, saving himself for me in those days? Actually, I *can* answer that, it was both because during the sex abuse years, Rose had their daughter, in approximately 1972.

I was developing at an early age and was showing an already heavy chest at the age of about 9 yrs. I was a real Tomboy, so wearing bra's was totally out. I hated it and I didn't want anyone else to notice my changes.

Most times that I was at Rose's flat, I'd be stared at by both of them and he'd say "B'Jesus, they're getting bigger than yours Rose!" I'd sulk because I didn't even want them! *and* because they're looking at them.

My 'bumps' hurt, they were hard, and to rub insult into this, dad got his fingers round them or one, and squeezed, saying "Cor bloody 'ell Rose, they're fucking rock hard!", and they'd laugh about it. She did eventually say, "Ahw leave 'er alone marty", (which isn't his real name, it's what she nicknamed him) I remember being near to tears about it. I had words screaming in my head, like, "Just get off me!" but my mouth wouldn't say it.

How many times should I have voiced out at him!? If I'd shouted at him the first time he made me touch him, I could've saved myself years, or countless incidents of sexual abuse.

It's seen as wrong, or unacceptable, for a child to tell the parent off, or mouth out at them…But it's not wrong, and it needs to be acceptable.

All children should have their voice heard and believed. Every perving parent, uncle whoever, should be named and shamed. I wish I had a voice then.

I couldn't tell him off, because he's 'dad', and as much as I didn't like what was going on, he wasn't going to stop, because I said 'No' in N London. I said 'No' in the bathroom, bedroom and living room in the flats. If only I'd shouted! Fucking yelled it from the roof tops! Maybe, maybe dad wouldn't have touched me ever again. Maybe dad wouldn't have forced me to sexually satisfy him over and over again.

I didn't tell people, well, I did tell a couple later in life. I didn't tell people about it then, not just because it was 'our secret', but initially, because I was silently, full time overwhelmed.

This was my first awesome, going round in my head as I went to sleep, and on waking up, to then attempt a normal day through school, daydreaming about it, and to go home, for more.

Still at Roses' flat after school, and it's one of those silent days of awe, and wondering where my Mum is.

Rose' was busy in her living room. Dad told her I was tired. He took me to Rose's' bed, and shut the door. I knew what to expect, but didn't really feel he would approach me in that way, but sure enough he dared to do it, and lied down next to me. Dad put my hand round his penis and made me sexually satisfy him again. I can't remember how he cleaned up, probably on another snotty, nicotiney handkerchief. I don't understand Rose not coming in, or at least asking why I wasn't sent home for an early night, or why dad was in there with me for a while. I went there for a nice dinner, and would've liked some attention like asked about school, but all I got, was dad putting on me yet again for sex.

I was slightly tearful, and mouth quivering. It wasn't because I thought I was doing wrong, because again, I didn't feel it was wrong, but more because it's me and dad and it's sex again. . I wasn't fucking tired either!

No, I wasn't tired, I felt mentally exhausted! Like mental sabotage, doing sex with dad nearly every time I saw him, then thinking about it all during school. My head had inner turbulence with thoughts of "dads' willy, then that sticky wet liquid from it, dirty handkerchiefs and my own dad pushed his willy into my crotch on our settee", and later, after school, being back there in reality, with another round of it all with him, to return to school the following morning, to daydream the previous nights' events, again, with that rape flashing around my head amongst the new stuff going on. And no one's telling me if I'm going to see Mum again!

He's one filthy, lying bastard, who knows exactly what he done to me, every touch, every calculated move, upon my five to fifteen year old body.

Dad And Roses' House
1972 To '75

DAD HAD MOVED into Rose's' flat. The Stepsister appeared approximately 1972, and I really didn't care. Then dad and Rose got the house near our flats.

Mum, brothers and I had moved to a house in Kent. I grew into my teenage years with not as much contact with dad thankfully…He was busy paying their mortgage by then, and serving the upkeep of Rose's' sons and now their daughter. We were abandoned by him. There was the rare contact, only when dad wanted to.

Out of the blue, at their request, I was asked to baby sit the Stepsister, which is a laugh because I was inexperienced with children, and certainly far from any maternal instincts. Some older siblings, have a natural caring and maternal way about them, but no not me. I was there for the money and fags.

I'd arrived there mid- afternoon, and well in time for tea. Within the first hour, after a cuppa, we were all standing and chatting in the kitchen. Stepsister was playing under and around the table, set back in a recess behind me. Dad then ogled at my breasts, grimacing, whilst breathing in through his mouth with a hissing sound, then saying "Cor look at them two Rose'". Dad got his fingers and thumbs over the top of them and applied some pressure, then saying "Bloody 'ell Rose'!", so that he can remind her that they were bigger and very firm. I was kind of used to it, but could never raise my voice to tell dad once and for all to fuck off!!', then go on to pulverise his head into a wall. My face must've said enough because Rose actually screeched at him about it, "Will you stop doing that, fucks' sake Marty, she don't want you grabbing her tits and embarrassing 'er, any time you bleedin' well see her!", That was a first for her, and support for me! Dad said "alright", which I think meant sorry? Dad was red. Dad was embarrassed. Good!

Late afternoon to evening, before they went out, dad had shown me the bedroom i'd be in, at the back of the house, then showed me their bedroom and Stepsisters' room. It was all obvious really. Rose's' sons had all moved on by this time. A short while after, and back downstairs, dad asked me to pop into their bedroom and get something out of their dressing table draw. The one he told me to go to, had a vibrator in it, and the draw didn't have what I was asked to get. Dad came up and opened that draw again, and looked at me, in that way as if to say, do you want this. (that vibrator) I took my eye contact off him and said "Well I couldn't find it" and walked off. Dad just never stopped perving on me! Creepy bastard!! It was around these times, when dad and Rose wanted me to go nude or topless in a sauna with them, and he was *still* grabbing my then even bigger breasts in that place any visits I done since!

A couple of years down the line, they all cleared off to Carlisle, then down to Wiltshire, where I visited from Kent a couple of times.

Relationships

I'm rubbish at relationships. Well I might as well be honest from the start.

The Older Man

My first relationship was when I was straight out of finishing secondary school, 1977 and seeing a guy aged 33. He was married and had just finished seeing some other woman he was having an affair with immediately before his wife learned about me. I took the brunt of all the playing away he done, by being blamed for their divorce, having things slung at me in the street and being called 'slut' every time his ex-wife saw me, even though we'd only recently met. I didn't know her feelings. I only saw her as some dragon who had kept picking on me and I was going to punch her if she kept on.

I was 16 years old, riding motorbikes, and didn't have empathy or feelings for his wife and kids. My 'parents' had divorced, so it was natural, and this was how I saw it. I didn't know any different. I was gone wild, flown the dysfunctional nest, living with a, by now, divorcee who's double my age, I was drinking like a fish out of water, and riding motorbikes all over the country. I wasn't planning to go garrity like I did, I just lived into my newfound freedom wildly, loving the growth of the bike group and the adventures of the weekends, but I wasn't trusting some other young women within it. Looking back at this mistrusting behaviour, I realise I devoted my time to it. During this mistrust, I was a miserable cow who at times created an atmosphere, what a killjoy I almost became. I don't think I was as possessive and mistrusting when I was properly drunk.

I'd nag this elder partner of mine 'G' behind the scenes about anyone I thought he's interested in and if she was top heavy, my world was ended because my mind was made up that he'd definitely shag her.

I was top heavy in my younger years, so in my mind, he'll sleep with any other top heavy woman. I hated the thoughts I had of him sleeping with another woman, and the more people in the bike world we met, the more I was convinced he's going to contact them and sleep with them if any one of them had a top heavy good figure.

This was such an inward torment to myself, but I couldn't trust anyone. These thoughts only ever escalated. On a rare occasion my thoughts mellowed if I'd spoken to a woman I'd previously kept a watchful eye on. I'd learn more about her, and mellow if she's with a guy who she is really happy with.

We often had the bike group round our house for the weekends or when we all came back from a rally. We'd nearly all be drinking and every one of us having a laugh, and even during these fun times, if G went into another room and was gone more than ten minutes, my head would be telling me he's being sexually satisfied by whatever woman I can't see in this room now, and other friends are keeping an eye out to warn him if I make my way out to find him, so that I won't catch him at it. There was a few times when I'd caught up with him, and he *was* chatting away with some other woman, so I'd go and chat with her guy, but I was still reeling about G going off for a chat with her, so my concentration on chatting with her guy was hit and miss because I was still having my mental riot and keeping my eyes on G.

We worked together in an industrial laundry near our house. He was the Manager. There was a lovely group working there, mainly Indian women. The few English women were of similar age to me. I had heard G's ex-wife used to work there. I was so mistrusting that one of the girls I worked with, looked like a younger version of the ex-wife. I'd watch them chatting and worked it out that he could well fancy her even though she's not top heavy, but because of her looks. Then it might've been a few weeks later, one other girl who usually dressed tidy in trousers, top and cardigans etc, suddenly turned up in t shirt and jeans, and she had a really slim waist and very firm looking large bust, so my fear of G fancying the ex-wife lookalike, immediately went onto the new busty one for months.

There's no getting away from my possessiveness, and mistrust.

I had a shock to my mistrusting mind in the end.

We were all at my 21st birthday party mid- November and had a disco in the back room of a pub we frequented in Rochester Kent.

A fight broke out between the pub governor and us in the back room, and he fired tear gas over us. G slung the sweet jar sized, jar of pickled onions into the disco deck. One thing led to another and in the chaos G asked me if I minded him giving S a lift home on his bike because her guy had cleared off. I was fine about it because I'd been chatting and drinking the few times we'd all met up, and I was really in my element because I was having a row, proper drunk, and in my heavy eye make-up, lipstick and black leather mini skirt and fishnet stockings and high heeled boots above the knees, a vest and no bra's. I was feeling real good about myself!

I rode from Rochester to Dartford, on my Honda CB 250 and waited for G to get back. This was to my mums' house because the laundry had closed down and we lost the tied tenancy. No sign of him all night. He'd slept with S that night. He told me I could still have him if I shared the bed with them, which I did, and we were going to stay like that, but I had other motives, thinking I'd win him back that way. I failed, and left them because life was about *them* and I was excluded throughout the house, meals and shopping etc.

Another day another bikers' disco in Rochester or Hoo Kent, and I'd seen them really happy together, and frankly rubbing my nose in it. My remaining friends and some who'd left the bike group because of what they'd done to me, were not happy. All the women I mistrusted and thought he'd sleep with, were my friends. I never suspected S to sleep with him, she's even younger than me. It all flooded back, about the being used by them, which was the final push, so I punched her eyes black and gave her a split lip. The fact that I mistrusted him in the first place was tormenting enough, but even with my eye on him, he still cheated, and didn't help me learn to trust anyone in the future either.

I had two more failed relationships between the stated two, but they're the same old story with the mistrust.

NEVER AGAIN WITH BLUE EYES.

It was 2014, we had a lot in common, this guy and I. We'd become close over the year. He's been a great listener to my upsets, anger and all, and to be honest, my stresses were consistent. I'd had a couple of near melt downs, when he'd turned up at my request, listened, hugged and encouraged.

He somehow half talked me out of getting my revenge on my dirty dad. This book is what really stopped me.

I did kinda love this guy but was definitely not 'in' love. We felt like soul mates during those days. We'd agreed, relationships aren't based on sex and our friendship is more important than sex.

So what was it like during intimacy? He was an affectionate guy. He held me firm yet tender, I looked at him, we kissed. I was on his left and laying on my right to be held closer to him. The lamp was on, on the dressing table behind him, which creates slight shadows on his face. I felt wanted.

There was another eye contacting moment, then a force of terror just engulfed me. I uncontrollably withheld my breath, and stared at his mouth instead, I withdrew from his hold, and said 'sorry'.

But I wasn't thinking 'sorry'! What the hell did I say that for? All I was thinking was 'Fuck off! Get out! Die!

He asked "What's up?". I told him "It's not you, sorry, I can't look at your eyes". He was genuinely concerned. He said "That's ok, you're fine, but why can't you look?".. I butted in (like I do), said "Sorry, I know you're *you* in bed with me but your eyes are my dad's, when we had eye contact, I was back in bed with *him* again. He said "Stop saying sorry, it's understandable after what went on.

He asked me if I wanted him to leave. I told him "No, I don't want you to leave".

But I didn't want him in my bed with me! I wanted to gouge those horrific eyes out!

I asked "Can we swap sides so that you've got the lamp lighting up your face properly?", which we did. It was no better really because the thin crease in his eyelids, over the same colour eyes as my dad's, morphed this guy into my dad lying next to me. I did find myself looking at his mouth and chin after that shattering flashback.

Another night soon after that previous horrific experience, we're under the duvet. All was going as good as it gets. Then dad had to turn up in my head. I was back on the settee in the flat, aged 6. I know it's this guy, but this has got to stop! Or I'm going to hurt him. I want to punch him in the head or kick him, just to stop it! I was about to yell something out like 'No!' but thankfully, I yelled out his name. Knowing what had just probably gone through my head, he stopped immediately and said "It's ok Eliza, It's me, you're alright". I was apologising yet again.

My real me was full of savage-like anger I wanted that savage anger used for revenge on dad even more after that.

There was another night, which was probably the decider for him, because he doesn't want to put me through the bedtime mental challenges that kept happening, and always says, "Sex isn't everything, there's more in friendship than sex, and once the sex is over, it's almost forgotten about, friendship is more important and I don't want to use you"

It was a decider for me because in my bed, I'd started on him, and as he was getting aroused, I flashed back. I was with dad in his bed again, doing what I used to have to do. As soon as we stopped, I had to turn away from him, because he was dad still, and I actually wanted to get up and clear off out, but I froze with the horrific flashback stuck with me.

He offered to not come round again in case we ended up in bed. I said "No, still keep popping round, or have you met someone else?" "No" he said, "Told you, I wasn't even looking for anyone, you turned up and I fell for you, I really want you, you're genuine, you don't drink and smoke, you make me smile and laugh, and you make it worth going to work for every week". Ah well, as convincing it all seemed, I'm still not able to trust anyone anyway.

The reduction of bedroom visits, was acceptable, we're both ok about that. However, the conversation did crop up very recently about sleeping together again.

I struggled to explain to him "Erm, I feel like I can't have a guy in my bed anymore. It's not you, you know that. All past relationships, there's always been some reminder of my dad but I was younger, drinking alcohol like a fish out of water, I suppose I managed to push the abuse to the back of my mind. I still have flashes of him and the inside the flat etc. For some reason, it's worse with you, your eyelids and hairline, are similar. Now dad is grey haired, your hair is similar under the lamp light. You're also similar in body and strength etc. It's happening with dad again while we're intimate. I have full intentions of completing bedroom stuff with you, and enjoying every second of us, then dad just appears and he's the one holding me, in place of you.

If I ever bother sleeping with anyone again, it'll probably be with a woman, definitely no one with blue eyes ever again. I know for a fact, I won't be having another blue eyed man in my bed again, or in my home overnight, sorry, really sorry, I just can't do the bed bit again."

He totally understood me, telling me "Eliza, it's alright, I'm not here *to* jump into bed with you, what we've had, has been the best, do I still want your body? Of course I do! But I love you for who you are. The bedroom bit might come back later when you've had a few visits to the Psychologist, but even if it doesn't, it won't matter, because we have a great friendship, and that matters more than sex". He was equally understanding about my mistrust issues, very patient with me too. I'd usually end up apologising to him for cross questioning him, and all he'd say is "Yes, I do feel it's getting a bit much now, but I know it's not your fault, because you've been abused by the very person who you was meant to be protected by, and he cleared off with your mums' best friend, you're probably never going to be able to trust anyone, but with this CPS thing going on and you feeling like your dad is laughing at you about it, you're doing the right thing by not getting your revenge, and writing instead. You'll get there, I know you will, I know you can't see it, but you've been at your worst moment, and you're turning it round. You'll get there babe".

We went our separate ways. I've not bothered looking for any relationships since".

Begun Writing...

During 1999/2000, India (My Daughter) was 6 years of age. It seemed as soon as she turned 6, I started re-living the abuse. I was consumed by it, living a 24/7 shock.

We were on speaking terms with my dad, but any days before he was due to visit us at our home also in Wiltshire, I used to warn India to not sit on his lap when he comes round..

It would be too close for mental comfort, and one false move, then I'd have to kill him, because that was just how I felt with this horrendous amount of dirty, disgusting everything, going round in my skull. I mean everything. His hands, fingers, eyes, voice, b.o, nicotine and smoke smells, the whole lot was within me, like one of those elastic band balls, that grows ever larger, and this was every hour of the day and through the night when I was awake.

Shortly after his last visit to us at that house, I couldn't face my dad anymore. It was too much for me to keep getting all the filthy reminders of dad. I made some phone calls and eventually arranged to take India and I to a womens' refuge in North Wales, to avoid seeing dad at my door, and him seeing India.

I was already feeling tired, and not used to travelling so far, so by the time we arrived there, I was totally exhausted. We had a nice welcome, and as soon as we were shown our room, I started preparing for bed.

Even though I was relieved to be out of our house and area, I felt something was wrong, like a spooky feeling. India was alright under these tiring circumstances thankfully, but I felt a need to run out of there. I was actually feeling scared. I tried telling myself it's tiredness, but the fear was stronger. I told India we'd get to sleep straight away, and leave as early as we can in the morning... Will we ever settle!?

As if I didn't have enough going in and out of my mind, I started worrying about the choice I was making, whether I can confront dad any time after returning home, or stay in the refuge room, (which I'd decided was haunted), for however long. Now there are two evils I'm scared to face up to. I kept jumping awake all night, startled by this eerie something and panicking about India, so kept checking she's still breathing. She was in my bed this night. So after another rough night, we left there at five am, and drove back through those bleak, slate mountains and drove towards home. My mind was in a hell of a mess.

On the way back, we stopped at the service station. I had been thinking over coffee break, about phoning dad, to give him a piece of my mind. One minute I thought, we'll just go home, act like nothing's happened and go back to the usual. Na can't. I can't stand him, and don't want him near me or my girl.

I walked from my car with India, over to the phone box just outside the services main doors. I was breathing heavier for the adrenaline and anger, which drove me to do it.

I dialled, he answered. Me "It's me & India". Him "Oh hello how are you's?". Me "Not good, I've decided I don't want you contacting us any more, right?". Him "Oh ok, what's up, are you feeling down?". Me, "Yeah, about my shitty past with you". Him "Well, I'm sorry, and if you don't want me to contact you, then I'll respect your wish". Me "You *do know* what I'm talking about don't you, with me and you?" Him "Yes I do". Me "Right, well don't contact us again". Him "Ok whatever you wish". Phone down... I was filled with awe but with a worry of him turning up to talk about it.

On our return to home, exhausted, and belongings half unpacked, India was dancing around, I was badly in need of a cup of tea and feet up. The water company guy knocked to tell me he has to show me how fast a dial is moving on the water metre, because my water usage is very high. I really didn't need him there right then. I've just driven back from a haunted room in Wales, after hardly sleeping I'm looking at something down a hole out the front of my house, Two neighbours decide to see what's going on, and India slams the front door, locking us out.

One helpful neighbour got up on a ladder and busted his way through a window, then got our front door open for me, and he kindly fixed the window for me, I don't know what happened to the water company guy. Those long two days were just the start of a downhill spiral.

I was still having counselling, when one night, I had the worst nightmare/re-surfaced memory, take over me. In this nightmare, I'd had a dress on, and was sat back on the settee, me as a six year old again in the flat, ready for a 'wrestling match' with dad. I knew what dad was going to do. He was going to blow raspberries gradually up my bare legs, then onto actually licking my vagina, but this resurfacing memory, kind of nightmared into dad approaching my India to abuse her!

He was blowing raspberries on *her* upper legs, and onto *her* thighs, then was about to lick *her* vagina, There was no shouting myself awake from this, or screaming any voice out to tell him to leave India alone and I had no voice to warn her. It was a sudden jolt of my head, which threw me awake and the nightmare had triggered that memory of what actually happened to me, when he ended up licking my vagina when I was six.

The whole following week or longer, was surreal. I felt in a permanent state of shock about it. Even during the counselling. It was as if I'd had a head injury, but forced to cope like everything is normal, and I felt like I was talking and sometimes moving in slow motion.

Every time India asked me a question, I'd snap back at her, and I hardly, if at all, spoke to her for a week, maybe a bit longer. I couldn't fit communicating with her, into my head, because she was so young that I usually needed explain my answers to her, which was impossible then, because I couldn't complete a whole thought.

I couldn't function with my usual orderly routine. Routine was gone. I was looking at people I knew, like I'd just dropped in from another planet, because that's what I felt like since that memory was horrifically slung at me.

Some nights, I'd be in our back garden gone 3am, still trying to complete thoughts, but nothing came together, apart from wanting to end it all.

Our back garden was only ten feet by ten feet walled at one side and fenced the other side and back, with a gate to our parking space. I'd be sat out there on a dining chair in the early hours, smoking one roll up after another, trying to think something through, anything, just wanted to stay on one subject. All I kept thinking was dad's head between my legs, having visions of the living room, where it happened in the flat, and thoughts of "Kill the cunt!'

I couldn't take any more of this overload of shock and anger, so decided to end it all.

With all the incomplete thoughts bursting in, then vanishing, I couldn't even begin to decide how to kill myself. There were so many subjects flashing in and out of my mind, that I couldn't hold onto any of them. It was like a pie chart, with 20 to 30, portions, each of which was a subject of a past incident or something else that was grim.

I couldn't work out a way to end it all. As soon as I got on the subject, it stopped. I couldn't think of one of the various ways to do it. I started to write each subject down as they rose to thought, then I jotted down a bit more because I managed to hold on longer to some subjects while seeing them on paper. Gradually, as more nights were turning to days, I had written tens of pages, from snippets of random subjects, then going deeper into some thoughts as they returned, and eventually, doing page after page of the sexual abuse, my feelings, and incidents by other perpetrators, along with all the other junk rumbling on in my head.

That was the start of me writing this book but I had to push on with life and seek work, because I wasn't affording anything with being a lone parent without maintenance.

Eventually, with more of my thoughts jotted out, my mind became more occupied with a new job and increasing valuable Mumma time with India.

I kept my writing packed away for the past eighteen years, which brings me forward to these days.

Dad 2009/12

It's June 2012, India and I having been living in rural South Wiltshire for three years to that date. We're living 6 miles from dad. Rose' has now passed on. For several years before this, India and I lived in Kent.

This is one of those phases of being on talking terms with dad, who I'd had years of talking with, then we'd have bad fall outs and not talking again for a few years. So here we are at this date, on talking terms again.

During these times, some Sundays, and the odd week day, dad would be at our house for dinner. India and I were very often helping him out with the strenuous gardening tasks, runs to the recycling centre, hospital runs, house cleaning and ironing etc etc.

Initially, when he started visiting us, he'd bring some sort of sweet contribution, and ask India how she was, and vice versa. India, during these 3 years, wasn't socialising, but would manage a show of being relaxed and ever respectful towards her Grandad, and worked well to put any anxiety she then had, out of sight.

When he had got used to the regular visits here, things became more relaxed, likewise when we went to his place. With this now, half relaxed atmosphere between us, he started saying a few more things which had India & I questioning once he left. Usually India would be the one to pick up on something he's said, first.

First off, as he entered our house, we'd greet him then India stayed in the living room whilst I made the coffees and briefly spoke with him in the kitchen. He'd ask me if India's allowed a snack or treat before dinner, usually a small chocolate bar and I would go with the flow, and thank him, like all's normal. We would be watching tv during and after dinner. He would often criticise what a woman is wearing, or go on and on about the news, slagging someone off, boringly so for the next hour. If it was news of someone been imprisoned for a sexual offence, I'd play it very cool, and act like nothing ever happened between us. I'd have to say *something* though, like, 'needs shooting', I couldn't just stay quiet. So, we kept listening to his views and criticisms, week after week.

He began to notice India looking a bit different, y'know, like teenagers do, hair colours, make- up and clothing styles etc. But he wouldn't say, "Something's different, oh, that looks nice India" if he was sure there was something different. Like when she'd lightened her hair for the first time. It looked lovely, from a light auburn to a soft, creamy blonde and it looked fresher. I confirmed to him India had lightened her hair, adding "Looks lovely doesn't it". His reaction was, "What have you gone and done to it!?", then, before we could say anything, he said, "Tch, they, (yes 'they') just can't leave their hair and faces alone these days can they!".

India was very let down about that, and I said, "No, it looks good and suits her really well". India was terrified of his reactions to any of her changes, to the point that even I started to worry, yet pull faces at him and laugh when he wasn't looking. We could see he was happy with himself for moaning about and criticizing India. I couldn't look at him because I was totally pissed off, yet i'd still never really had a proper go at him face to face about anything. As we walked in the living room, I got eye contact with India, and rolled my eyes, then gave an evil behind his back. That was just one of the first times he'd criticized her.

Another time he lacked compliments, was about her having her nose pierced, India looks good with it, she has the look, which suits any style. He said, "Ah, it looks ok" in a moody attitude and didn't compliment it at all. As annoyed as I was getting with his unnecessary criticisms, I'd half hoped he'd one day just shut up, or India would blow a stack and put him out the door, but over time, he carried on with his nasty attitude and India remained respectable and continued to deal with her anxiety, whilst it all boiled within me.

He was due round on another Sunday, midday. India and I were looking forward to our massive roast dinners, but as for dad/Gtandad, we was fast losing that welcoming feeling, for tension, at wondering what the hell he'd be moaning at India about next. She said, "What if he moans at me again mum?" I told her "I don't know what to say, cos he moans all the time, but i'm not having him picking on you like that anymore".

The usual hard bang!, bang! at the front door. India and I quickly glared at each other, with a silent mutual "Here goes". I bunged the kettle back on, whilst India let him in. Straight into the kitchen he'd head, for a peck on the lips and hug for both India and I. That too was

49

a regular greeting and a goodbye, and as soon as it happened, I'd often smell a flashback of bed with him.

India had sorted the TV or dvd to play, and the smallest of nest of tables for him, and he sat down in the 'joey' chair, our brown leather armchair. She collected his cup of coffee from the kitchen. I heard him say "Thank you darling". Then, less than a minute later, he chanted "Why do you wear those jeans like that? They look bloody stupid!" You know that style of the baggiest flares, too long for their leg length and dragging along the floor? That was what she had on but who the fuck did he think he was to roar his opinion in her face like that!?

Even before he'd finished his controlling, orderly opinion, he was making his way back in the kitchen, still continuing to try completely shaming India, who stayed in the living room. Under my breath, I sighed a 'fuck me, what now!', whilst slamming the gravy jug down on the work top. He hurts me when he hurts Indias' feelings.

I retorted, "Stop having goes at her! What has she actually done wrong for you to keep having goes at her every fuckin' week!? She's a teenager! She's not out doing drugs or beating people up! Ain't it enough, that she has no social life because of others bullying her? She used to look forward to seeing you, and now her own fuckin' grandad is denting her confidence!"

I was totally stressed, and felt immensely sorry for India, and guilty for allowing this miserable, conceited and perverted, dirty old git into our home, to hurt my closest one. He actually apologised and became tearful. I didn't apologise for my outburst though. He started talking to India, treating her more grown up and kind'f showed a bit of respect to her after that. I spoke like nothing had happened until he left. India didn't smile at him anymore that day. I don't blame her. He was becoming overcritical, and seriously looking for something to moan about. India hadn't heard exactly what I said during my outburst, but I told her, and that it made him cry. She was surprised, yet still pressured about him visiting, and us visiting his place. I was developing a feeling that our visits to each-others' homes were going to stop in the not too distant future anyway but had no idea how.

To earn a bit of pocket money from her Grandad, India used to muck in at his house, by hoovering through and wiping round the bathroom, whilst I would iron up to 14 shirts, and sometimes the bedding.

His place is a two bedroomed park home, like a 'kit form' bungalow, where the single and double bedrooms have a fitted wardrobe at the foot of the beds. Walking round the bed to change the bedding, wasn't actual walking, it was side steps due to the lack of room.

It seemed to be becoming a regular thing, for India more often so, sometimes myself, to get cornered in his bedroom when he wanted his bedding changed. He used to always make some excuse to need to get past her by the foot end corners of his bed. In the end, she'd wait back or just walk quickly towards the door, then let him get in, and back out again before she'd go back in there. There was no room for anyone to pass each other round the bed. He would always do that awkward move when we were in there. We didn't want to run across his bed. One, that's a fab excuse for him to whine and lecture us. Two, the less we touched his bedding with his shedded dead skin over it, the better we felt.

One day, I had to do that side step shuffle, to get past him at one foot corner of the bed, and as straight as I could make myself, I couldn't avoid a light brush of contact with him of my butt against his crotch. I instantly flashbacked, and felt like he was going to stroke his fingers from my crotch up to the top of my butt, and hear that sound, which he used to make, like a trumpet, with his tightly closed thinned lips, like when he used to run his fingers over my vagina after a bath, and like he used to do to Rose, against her clothing over her butt, in front of us, like she was some kind of trophy. I mean what the fuck was I meant to say or do when he done that to her!? What was India meant to say or do!? We are females, even though I've rarely acted like one. We wasn't interested! Anyway, yes, I flashed back to that sound and feeling during brushing past him.

Fact is, I should never have been *his* property, to be 'touched' and 'put', like some item he owns. Clearly, he believed I was, and god help him if he really thought my India was next in line for his sexual frills and satisfaction whilst she was doing his cleaning or otherwise.

Well, it wouldn't have taken off because if India hadn't put him through a wall first, I would have. This bedroom, 'merry dance' wasn't the only dread either. It was much like the ironing board issue, yes, another regular reason for him to be contentious, and plain old pervy

51

Dad used to make me wonder to myself whether I'd snap and murder this perverted bastard. .

The kitchen is what you walked into as you enter dads' front door. It's a square kitchen, with the door opposite leading to the hall, bedroom and living room etc. It was always very clean, like the rest of the place, very neat and organised looking. I used to enter, then bung the kettle on, make us a cuppa. Oh, and that kiss and hug would've happened by now. I'd take his cuppa and baccy into him in the living room, where he would've been watching some jaw droppingly boring black and white oldie on tv, and we'd be given the rundown on it, and we'd say "Oh yeah?", whilst gritting our teeth to stifle our yawns, and attempt to look genuinely interested. India and I would have drunk our drinks quickly, then crack on with the duties.

I would be ironing away in the kitchen, and he'd make an appearance and start chatting away. He'd be standing at the end of the sink work top near the front door, and opposite me, smoking a roll up, but instead of chucking that finished roll up out the front door or in the ashtray next to him, he'd decide to go behind me to get to the bin, which was under the work top to my right. He'd by brush past and against my arse, very lightly. I didn't know whether to make him believe I didn't feel him against me, let him know that's too fuckin' close and pick the ironing board up and shuffle forward, and slam it down, or just go the whole hog, and stove the iron into him. Well, I looked round to my right, and he was crouched down at the bin, like nothing happened but he had to brush back past me, so I shuffled me and the board forward, then back, as soon as he got past. He said stroppily "Well why do you have to be with ye back right against the work top?" I said "because it's comfortable to lean back on it, and more room in front of the ironing board"..

I know! I didn't have the guts to say "Cos you brush against my arse and I don't fuckin' like it!"

So the mood continued, and India cracked on with her duty as quickly as possible in order for a quick escape.

Another time, when he was sent to try us…

He came into the kitchen, filling it with smoke from his roll up. I mentioned about my eyes stinging, which he questioned. I repeated it, adding "I hope it don't make your shirts smell smoky or nicotiney". Dad said "What ye on about? There's hardly any smoke in here!" already in one of his moods. "Hardly any!?" I blurted out, "There's a blanket of the stuff look!" Then he stormed outside and slammed the door, saying "Uh right, i'll fuckin' smoke outside then!" I looked through the open hatch from the kitchen to the living room, India was looking over to me startled, asking "What's that?". I told her "It's him bellowing smoke all over me, I'm pissed off with it and he's got arsey with me".

We made tracks quickly after that. I rapidly started walking off straight to the car, India got stuck in mid-escape for the 'ritual' of the kiss on the closed lips and the big hug. Yes, every time we'd be ready to leave there, he'd wipe his thin yukky aged lips dry, and we had to give him a big tight hug and closed mouth kiss on the lips.

Loads of times when we'd leave there and driving off, I'd think, 'why do I do that?' and 'I don't like it' and 'How do I stop that bit?' Week after week, into the months, it gradually became more of a cringe feeling.

I'm sure he thought I hadn't any realisation of his 'gentle perving', which was all I *did* see it as. This little ironing board move started becoming too regular, and he'd often say, "What is it about wanting the ironing board so close, you've no room between the worktop and yourself?" I then got into the habit of picking the lot up and shuffling forward, so that he didn't touch me.

I decided to start setting the ironing board up as soon as we'd arrived, whilst asking him if he wanted anything from that corner or in the bin, before I started. When I first done that, he was not happy, saying "You're bleeding keen aren't ye?" I told him "Yeah it's best I cracked straight on with it, so that when I sit down, I don't have to start work when I get up again". He couldn't argue with that, even though I still had to shuffle forwards on the odd occasions.

It became a regular thing to attempt those snidey little moves. I used to think, 'Does he think I've forgot all about the sex between us when I was a kid, then maybe he's going to attempt to perv on me, like it's something new?' Or does dad think I've remembered the sex between us, and trying me out, to see if I want to resume this dirty connection we had in the sixties and seventies?'

No part of this relationship of mine and dad's was to become any easier or even bearable. Him moaning, those near fuckin' lectures! had gotten to us over the months. He had gained nearly all mental control over me again, and now almost over India. I don't even understand myself, for not stopping the abuse and his control. I should've been one of those loud kids, who could make a stand, shout louder than he could rule, yet my bank of sentences, to paragraphs of rage, never left my tongue at him, apart from that day he harshly criticised and upset India.

What became a normality when we left dads' place, was the venting of my stress by yelling out "Y'know what, he can shove that place right up his arse!" I would be firing my seething anger out, at the fact that he's, "*lecturing us, after all he done to me!!*", then "Well he can fuck right off next time our phone rings, cos I ain't in! And next time there's a gas leak, I won't fuckin' smell it!" India, even though completely empathic with me, would roll up laughing at me, having changed from a fairly respectful, "Yeah bye dad love ya", to some screaming witch on overdrive. She'd then ask "D'you mean it mum about him shoving that place up his arse?", hoping I did, but for a year or so more, we kept having him round or we kept going to his place. We needed pocket money.

At home one evening, India gently and so carefully asked me; "Mum", me, "Yeah", India, "Y'know at grandads' house?" "Yeah". "Can we not do that kiss anymore?"

I said "Why's that?" India said, "Well, I don't really like it". I said "He's only being nice, I don't think he's being pervy". The minute I said that, I began to feel like he *is* controlling us, by giving us money, and that squeezy long hug isn't necessary, especially as we're only 6 miles apart. It's not like we're travelling back to Kent and not seeing him for months on end.

Yes, India is right, and I'm cringing about it anyway. I told India, "I know he'll definitely get a strop about this one, but the next time we're there, I'll tell him". I added, "You're right actually India, sorry", and "I wonder if because of what I went through with him years ago, is maybe why I didn't see that kiss as pervy as what it possibly really is, and to think about it, I don't think the step-sister even kisses him, if she does, it's only a peck on the cheek".

So, the next time arrived, and we're round his house, I'm halfway through the ironing, thinking, "shall I chat with him about it, or just blurt it out when the time comes? Either way, this could cause a serious strop". In the end, I had worried about it on and off, so bad, that I decided he can take it or leave it.

We don't owe him anything, and why should I be the one to feel like I have to kiss him on the lips, when I wasn't brought up by him. No, I wasn't *brought up* by him, I was abused, then abandoned by him really.

It was home time. He wiped his mouth and about to pout his lips and I said, "Oh!, India's gunna do just a peck on the cheek from now on, cos she's getting older now and to be honest, stepsister doesn't ever kiss you on the lips does she, so *we'll* just do the peck on the cheek from now". Sorted, all in one rambling mouthful! A bit harsh of me but hey, no more scratch-rough, nicotiny, damp, lip kiss no more! His chances of control are slipping rapidly from him. His head dropped down a bit and he rolled his eyes saying "Uh ok then".. That was mild compared to his latest behaviour.

I'd become a Market Trader. I was selling my own written designs, hand screen-printed onto babies hooded tops and all ages of t shirts. I was regularly trading in South Wiltshire markets, where dad would often show his face.

It was a Wednesday. I was trading in Amesbury. India had no college this day, so she traded with me, but after the first couple of wake up hours, where she'd helped me set up pitch, she returned to the car, living on her phone like teen's do..

Dad turned up, and realised India was in the car behind my pitch, and went to chat with her. She had previously expressed a couple of times to me, of how she's "Getting a bit fed up with him questioning me every time he talks to me". The day and trading moved on, and after packing down the gazebo, and car loaded etc, I drove us the 6 miles home.

By now, India was handling her anxiety really well, and even has a partner, and going out etc.

Not long after getting home, there was a call on the landline, I was busy sorting out my stock and finishing an order for the Fridays' trading in Warminster. India took the call, saying "Oh hi grandad, you ok?" whilst smiling initially, then started looking over at me with that 'What the fuck!?' look. I was starting to breathe heavier, and sorting my stock out, ever quicker, thinking, 'What could he want now? We only saw him about 6 hours ago India was saying bits of sentences around him obviously butting in, then she said, "Er yeah, ok? bye, love ya" Phone straight down.

Her face said enough, and I thought back to when I'd dropped some money off, which I owed him, when he kept broaching the subject about India and her partners' relationship. One time I'd gone round there and told him India won't be round because of no college, so she's having a lie in. Straight back at me he said, "Oh she's catching up on the night before with her partner?". I said "What, you mean are they having sex?" He said "I bet they are", in a still questioning kind of way. I said "I don't know and don't care either. It's none of ours or anyone else's business, and I ain't talking about it anymore".

Something was badly up, because India's always been respectful to anyone, including him, even though she knew about most of the abuse business, which i'd made her aware of, so that *if* we had ever ended up on our own at his place, we'd have a plan in place to avoid closeness to him. The way India said "Love ya" then just hung up, wasn't the usual India, she'd usually have said, "Love ya grandad, bye", in her usual chirpy and respectful way.

"What's up?" I asked. "I don't believe that!", India said, looking shocked. My stomach panged and felt my cheeks burning and heart racing. "Well he told me not to tell ya mum". "Oh fuckin' *did he now*?!" I sternly retorted. "He asked questions about me & ****** (her partner) again, then said don't tell your Mother I said that".

Oh boy! That's not a good thing for him to do because I instantly thought "Daddy's and Eliza's' secret", as if he was thinking he could do it to manipulate India, or getting off at the thought of it.

Thankfully India's better clued up to perv's and other dodgy people, than I'd ever been. She knew he was wrong to do that, and always tells me anything that she's felt uneasy about.

My heart was racing away with itself, my wrists went weak, and hands were shaking.

I thought, 'That's *really* fucking *it* now! NO MORE talking to him, ties cut permanently!' Determined this time because he'd extensively wound us up with his preaching of what's wrong or right way too often. This became the last, and I bloody well meant it.

It shouldn't be like this! A "Father", shouldn't make their offspring feel like you wanna kill the fucker! In the heat of this moment, rounders' bat and head were all I could imagine. We don't need this shit. I don't need *more* of his shit! I've had my share of the lowest, most revolting shit from him as it is. Don't! repeat it onto my beautiful girl. Get within arms' length, look at her, and you're gone!

Whether it's me picking him up by the throat, or India doing what she needs to, he won't be alive for breakfast. That's just what I was angry enough to do. I mean, who the hell did he think he is to preach to me!?... the very person he done those vile acts upon!?

That evening, and the following day, I was working flat out making new screens for Wednesdays' orders. They had to be done then because I was trading in Warminster on Friday. Thursday, I was printing, and sorting out stock, generally very busy.

I really didn't want him turning up at the pitch. I was very nervous and still bloody angry. Thinking, if he turns up, I'll tell him to 'Get the fuck, out of my sight, right now!', but facing him in public felt different, I'd probably really say "I know what you told India, and i'm not happy about it" but I can't do that either, it's too polite and weak for how I felt.

I decided to write a note on Thursday evening, I wrote several notes and trashed them due to straying from the point with anger, because of flashing back to the abuse I'd suffered over the years. Some notes were just not firm enough for how angry I felt. Eventually I got down on paper what he needed to read. I popped it through his letter box at 05:45 on the way to Warminster market.

I'D WRITTEN;

"Dad
Can you not go to Warminster today.
I missed that call, which India took last night, and again you asked her about hers and her partners' private life.
India and I are feeling very uncomfortable about it.
You're her Grandad, 80 years old – asking a 17yr old – Grandaughter basically if there's sex going on. It's inappropriate and pervy.

Whatever goes on in anyone else's private life, should stay there, in their private life.

India's been brought up to tell me everything, so that I can and could protect her from that crap I had as a child.

She told me, you told her not to say anything to me because "all that stuff is a taboo subject!". Again, that's wrong to make it look like _you_ can talk to her, about 'behaving herself' sex, or private life, whatever you want to call it, _and_ to do that behind my back.

If India feels a need to talk about anything like that, then she knows she can – with me – her Mum.

As you well know, my upbringing was wronged by you when I was living at our flat – you may choose to not remember. I never forget. India's upbringing <u>has </u>been <u>protected </u>and will be by her partner aswell.

Sorry it's come to this kind'f letter but I thought I made it clear several times before when you kept throwing questions & comments about it.

Eliza".

Some days after that note, I received a phone call from the eldest brother. We'd got into conversation, and dad was mentioned. I said "Yeah, well, I guess I'm disqualified from that will of his again". I said 'again' because, he had disqualified me from his will, a few years ago, because of one of our fall outs. The brother said "It seems like it yeah".. "You two (other brother) will help me fight it if I am disqualified won't you's". He said "Yeah, we'll give you a bit of ours". "No! I don't mean that, I mean to fight for what should be my share" He said something about he couldn't answer something like that there and then.

Some days after that, dad rang me, telling me I'm still going to be in his will, and it's going equally to us 6, which includes Rose's' 2 sons. Then he asked me about the letter I popped through his door. The words 'Oh fuck!' ran through my mind, as I crumbled at remembering mentioning about him acting pervy.

He said an excerpt from letter, then said, "..and about this bit you put about me being 'pervy', I'm not one of those bloody pervs, I haven't ever been like that, or touched you have I".

My weak and willowing nerves whipped away, leaving me about to erupt with raging anger at his attempt to intimidate me, into lying to myself, and to *still* keep it 'our secret'... Or was he actually daring to assume and hope i'd forgotten all that had happened? I said "Ohw come on dad!"

My breathing and heart thumps were fighting each other to be the loudest, and I thought, there's no point in covering it over yet again now. He said "What d'you mean?" in his tone of disagreement. I blew my stack and went for it, and said "What about what happened in Hampton Court!?" He said "You bleeding liar!". I hadn't even said *what* went on.

Well!, after everything, he put me through, for his sexual satisfaction, when he was 33 years of age, and I was 5, he dared to call me a bleeding liar when I hadn't even mentioned details of the abuse.

By now, my legs and arms were shaking, nerves jangled and shredded. So straight after he called me a 'bleeding liar', I gave him many years of anger with no holding back, It was still slightly scary, yet weirdly aggressive shit, but I raged on.

I said "What about the bathroom! and your bedroom! and Rose's' flat aswell then ay!?". He butted straight in and trying to yell out over me yelling out "You fucking liar!"

I hadn't even mentioned what actually went on between us! "You're the fucking liar!" I said,

He hung up, whilst still calling me all the lying whatever's under the sun. I was still f'ing and c'ing away at the now dead phone line. Him hanging up on me clearly shows his guilt.

My head and neck were instantly aching and tense, with just enough room in my head for the fear that my now heavily pounding heart was going to make a live appearance.

I was breathing like I'd just done a speed swim, with the driest throat, whilst trying to gulp air back into my lungs.

I felt an edge of awe for my eruption, with thoughts of, "I've fucked him off for good".

Then thoughts of the so called brothers and step sis are going to call me, or call round to punch my lights out", and in the next thought, "I'm not in that family anymore", and, "He was my own flesh and blood, we had sex, and that cunt just called my sex abused childhood a fuckin' lie!"

It was him calling me a "fucking liar", which pushed me to report those years of sex abuse to Wiltshire Police. I won't accept him abusing me for many years, sabotaging my childhood, adulthood, education, sexual relationships and ability to trust others, to then call *me* the "fucking liar"! just because I remembered it and lived with it all my life! Then he tells the rest of the family, "Uh, she's in one of her not talking moods again.

No! I was not in one of *those* not talking moods! Fact is, my truth was hurting you!

CID

Laura was my Investigating Officer from the CID, who arranged a video statement, and questioned me on video about my experiences as a victim of sex abuse.

Right from the start, she's been open, honest and matter of fact, and warned me the first few times we spoke, that we may not get charges because of possibly not enough evidence, and if there's any element of doubt of a successful prosecution, there'll not be a trial.

She worked with determination to gather every scrap of my medical history, researching for further written evidence of the sex abuse via contacts across Kent, Dorset and Wiltshire.

She questioned the rest of my so-called family, as well as dad himself. How does one start a conversation on that subject out of the blue? I know it's her job, but she's been on the victims' journey too, and believed victims throughout it. So the pathetic, lenient sentences from the successful prosecutions, and the cancelling of the trials, are equally gutting for her because she's the one who's been gathering the evidence of my journey for the duration of the case and works hard to fully present the evidence to the Crown Prosecution Service, in the hope of getting charges and successful prosecution of the perpetrators. I guess it's soul destroying when the huge effort she makes, falls to cancelled trials or given pathetic lenient sentences to those nonces and other sex criminals who ruin victims' lives.

She was few and far between on phone calls and visits, because other crimes and court sessions never stop, and the gathering of evidence for victims isn't a constant thing, but it's a lesson on patience. It's a long awaited process for documented facts, dug from archives, and tiny evidential snippets, picked out from bundles of paperwork. If that isn't frustrating enough, there's added pressure because of a time limit put on Investigators, to have the documented evidence to the CPS by. As soon as news of any evidence came in, Laura would let me know, and still warn me to not get my hopes up because it could all close suddenly, and no charges made.

Across a few months, with video statement done, research and further questioning, for clarification, there seemed to be a quiet time, whilst the Crown Prosecution Service sifted through it all, and asked Laura more questions.

I waited, and waited more, then, one evening, I received a phone call from another Detective Constable, explaining something about the charges. Charges? Laura had gone on leave, which is why he called me. He thought I'd been informed the previous week that they'd questioned dad, and have 12 charges against him, and dad didn't help himself during questioning.

It was 6 charges of Gross indecency with a girl under fourteen years of age, and 6 charges of Indecent assault on a girl under the age of 14 years. In my opinion, it's dozens of more charges, and attempted or maybe successful rape, but apparently, these cover the 10 or so years that it was happening.

We went to the Magistrates' Court, then Crown Court a few times, Laura told me I don't have to go to them, but me being me, just had to see dad in the dock. He looked as guilty as he knows he is, fidgeting around, concentrating more on me than looking and listening to the Judge, and dad actually smirked at me from the dock...and he reckons he's innocent.

Throughout each session, I think about three, maybe four sessions in all, in Wiltshire Law courts, the eldest brother turned up with his daughter, and another niece, and my step-sister, who all totally ignored my Daughter India, who has done nothing to offend them whatsoever.

The eldest brother, Mr know all, who didn't look as important as he liked to believe he was, had a laptop on in court, whispering to the others, all about what is right or wrong with what's been said.

He clearly knew jack shit, because he supported dad the pervert, whilst disbelieving me, holding the truth. Their general ignorance and the odd glare, made it clear the truth hurts.

They should try being in my shoes, actually experienced those sex acts, with that nonce right there in the dock, then to be called a liar by it!

I sometimes couldn't keep my mouth shut during the court sessions, and was told to be quiet several times by someone on my right, I think she may've been a Police Officer actually. It's ridiculous to hear the Judge, mentioning something about dad's age, in a way that one has to take it into consideration, so I raised my voice again, making it clear that dad "Didn't care about my age being 6 when he was trying to fuck me!" Making damn sure the so called family sat right in front of me, heard it too.

Laura and her colleague Dave, who I'd also had a good chat with in the waiting area, before the first court appearance, made India and I feel protected from the dads' supporters, ensuring we went out of the court rooms separately, and were kept at a distance at all times, which was unexpected, and a welcomed moment. Laura would then explain what the jargon all meant in each session, and what to expect from that, then she'd be dashing off to yet another case.

When she visited, she always explained why things change, and what went well etc. She said about some of her experiences, not individual cases, or names but stuff in general, which made me understand how much stress and upset can actually go on. There's probably 1 case in 10 that actually makes it to the final court sessions and prosecution. That's why she explains every step, whether it's been a good thing or seemed dodgy towards getting over the next hurdle, which there are many of. It's so bloody frustrating trying to get justice!

Laura totally believed me, and wanted to make sure justice is done for my sabotaged childhood, and a life that's been weathered by flashbacks, childhood sex acts upon me, and my almost out of body experiences, like haunting places. We want justice also, to prevent other young girls who could be at risk from my nonce dad.

I don't understand why we can't use a truth drug or lie detector tests in this day and age. It's been used on television programs. I read briefly, a snippet about the lie detector tests being tried in the Midlands, on sex offenders on licence etc. They should be used during questioning.

Laura again, has been more than the pressured job she does. She's understood where and what I've come from, with empathy. She carried on thinking of other ways to secure a prosecution by asking me anything she can follow up. As if that wasn't enough, she then went on to save my life by preventing my suicide going ahead

All in a days work ay. Thank you Laura.

I'd been informed by Laura, that for any reason, the case could be closed at any of the many hurdles that the judicial system meets, which I'd not liked, but nothing I could do about it. Some other group of legal people would be looking at the case again before a trial can be set, and they'd be discussing it with another Barrister.

From the previous court attendance in December 2013, and with the 'not' guilty plea, the Witness Care Unit, informed me it looks like the trial is definitely on because a date has been set for it.

A trial was set to begin in July 2014. Bloody hell, I'm going to get justice!

By February 2014, for some unknown reason, the trial date moved to August 2014.

During this time, I had put anything I could possibly remember as evidence, in writing, and dropped it off to Laura. I'd included a snippet about when I was raped at the age of 13, by a friends' Brother. It was a rant really, because I never got justice for it.

The CPS checked this out as I'd reported it not at the time of the rape, but I'd reported it later, twice, a few years apart. I had counselling for it because I was having flashbacks, nightmares, resurfaced memories, the whole shebang, for the rape and the sexual abuse.

Just to quickly explain something. During the second report in 2007 of the rape in 1973, I mentioned to the Met CID Investigator during him questioning me, I thought I'd seen one of the witnesses, months, maybe years before. (There was some friends with me when it happened). I'd added that it could've been one of the nightmares though. Whilst I was explaining everything to that Investigator, I felt the answers had to be at snap speed when being questioned, so as soon as I thought of the witnesses, I blurted it out.

Laura, investigating the sex abuse, came to my house in April 2014. As soon as she walked in, she said "Bad news I'm afraid Eliza". I thought, 'dad's died and bang goes my justice!". She said "The trial isn't going ahead". I still expected her to say he's a gonna, or words to that effect. She said "The Crown Prosecution Service picked up on some things you said, and they think it will undermine your case, and I've been arguing with them across the past couple of days".

She'd received a letter from them, which she brought with her, and I read, and she told me she was going to have to give me my copy of it on the following Saturday. All I could think of and say, was, "He ain't getting away with this", and "No, I'm not accepting this". I cried a bit but was more shocked. I just couldn't piece together any of the CPS's reason to make sense of it. Laura added, "I know it's not what you wanted to hear Eliza, and we've always known it could be stopped at any point". "I told her "I know, but I was lead to believe, once the trial had been set, it meant the Prosecution and Barristers etc, had everything finalised and once it's set, there's no stopping it". Laura said "I know exactly where you're coming from Eliza, and they've found something that they feel can undermine your case, and it isn't to do with this case, and it doesn't make any sense to me either". I said "Well I'm not having this, it's a load of bollocks! First dad calls me a liar, now this lot calls me one. After I read the letter, and unable to believe this news for a start, I then felt like they'd taken dads' side, and the whole justice system weighed against me.

I'd been open and honest, because there's nothing wrong with being open and honest when you're telling the truth right? Wrong.

The CPS cancelled the trial. I wasn't able to include their letters, but my argument follows on, which will clarify their reasons and the impact it had on me.

The CPS had received copies of the rape report, turned everything around and twisted it for good measure, and used this against me in my dads' case.

The CPS decided to stop the trial, basing their decision on me stating, "Seeing witnesses may have been a dream", they say "May undermine your case". One totally irrelevant incident, (which did happen) used against me.

But that wasn't enough for the CPS to push me down with...

Referring to the CPS's letter the collation of evidence, it's said that *I'd* said I was raped by ***my brothers' friend.*** This is what my counsellor reportedly stated that I'd said back in the 1970's. This tells the CPS, I'm not only saying I've been sexually abused and attempted rape by my dad, *and* claimed to have been raped by my friends' brother, which is all true, but the CPS have decided, *I'm now saying* I was raped twice. Once by ***my friends' Brother*** and once by ***a friend of my Brother.***

But they didn't ask for more information about some second rape like they did about the first. The CPS judged me on this written mistake.

There was I, genuinely thinking I'm getting some further help with justice via the CPS. Seriously, I actually thought they were seeking more evidence because they intended to help me. They were seeking this evidence to actually use it against me, which they did.

The 'one' rape by my friends' brother was 1973

The sex abuse and attempted rape by my dad, was from approximately 1964 on and off to 1975. They are two very different perpetrators, in different areas, at different times of my youth.

So they stopped the trial for the sex abuse and attempted rape by my dad because;

1. I'd said to the CID Investigator that "seeing my rape incidents' witnesses may have been a dream"... *"May undermine your case".*
2. I made a claim about a second rape by *"a friend of my brother"...* *"Clearly undermines you as a witness".*
3. It was questioned about the time scale from the *rape in 1973,* to reporting it in 1995, and on investigation, the named witnesses were unable to support the account provided, and in fact some

of them "contradicted the account". The Police decided to - No further action on the complaint on the basis that the account was not substantiated and may therefore be *'untrue'*.

For a start, those three points above, have absolutely nothing to do with my case against my dad, nothing!
And in answer to them;

1. Whether I had seen one of the witnesses or not. Doesn't mean I wasn't raped when I was 13 by my *friends' brother,* and around the time of me mentioning it to the CID investigator in 2007, I was suffering from flashbacks of that rape, and nightmares about the witnesses seeing me leaving the bedroom immediately after. Anyway, It's nothing remotely to do with the sex abuse and attempted rape trial, and I would've explained that to the jury.

2. I didn't ever claim to a second rape, by *any friend of any brother!* CPS made that decision, not me, and you based that decision on a written mistake. CPS went ahead with that decision without chasing it up with me or Laura first. Fact is...The *friend of my brother*, who I keep highlighting along with **my *friends' brother, is the same person... He, who raped me... once.* A mix up of words, and again, it's nothing to do with the sex abuse and attempted rape trial, and I would've explained *that* to the jury.

3. I explained the reason for the time scale between the incident and reporting it. I didn't know it was a reportable crime back in 1973, when I was 13. I did tell my mum 'J forced me to have it with him". Nothing was done about it. I saw a photo fit of a rapist local to my area, in 1995, which prompted me to report my rapist, who *is* definitely *a rapist...* and it *is true*! Yet again, it's nothing to do with the sex abuse and attempted rape trial and I, again, would've explained *that* quite easily to the jury... had I been given my day in court!

So that was what they based their decision on, to cancel the trial against my dad, nothing whatsoever to do with the case itself, and something not impossible to explain to a jury.

There are often questions flying through my mind about this, even now. I can't ask the relevant people because the case is closed.

- Why didn't the CPS chase it up with the Police if they believed I'd made a second rape allegation?
- Why throughout all this investigation, have I had to feel like I am the guilty one?
- What difference should it make to the trial whether I was raped once, twice or twenty bloody five times as long as I'm telling the truth!?
- Why, even when my dad didn't help himself during questioning by the Police, does the CPS still work *for* the perpetrator?
- Why, during a pre-trial hearing, did they mention dad's age, like it was going to be taken into consideration?
- How comes there was enough evidence to bring twelve charges against my dad, (should've been many more), yet the CPS dropped the trial when I mentioned another perpetrator? The case wasn't dropped because of insufficient evidence, like what the CPS usually state. Those 10 remaining charges still stood against my dad. Nothing changed them.
- Why didn't that un-empathic South London CID guy bother questioning J, the Kent rapist.
- Why punish me for being a victim of more than one rape. Multiple sex crimes do happen to victims and judgement shouldn't be dished out on victims for trying to get justice for them.

I hope I've made it clear enough to understand.

Several more argumentative letters went to and from the CPS.

The CPS eventually cut ties with me during this fight, telling me they'll not assist me any further and any correspondence will be filed without reply.

Sad to say, I'm not the only person to have a trial stopped. There's only approximately one in ten prosecutions actually get over all those stupid hurdles. I imagine all of us who can't get justice for the years of sex abuse, feel like the CPS have actually jeopardised our case's, for finding the slightest excuse to push a trial out of court.

I'm totally pissed off about it, and they know I am. The Police get pissed off about it as well, I know they do. They do all the research and investigations, then all that leg work is gone in a flash because of the CPS, just slinging our destroyed childhoods out of the judicial system. Then the Police and Investigators have to face us victims to tell us our one, long awaited chance of justice has gone.

The rest of the week, I was at work. I was a bit tearful on and off but mostly shell shocked about it, and believing the CPS think I'm attention seeking.

Laura was due round at 2pm, that following Saturday...

It's Saturday 12 April 2014, about 12:30... I'd decided this life really isn't meant for me. Sex abuse by my own so called dad throughout my childhood, and other incidents by other perpetrators have become the core of my life, and not only does dad call me a liar about his actions, so too are the CPS!. What *is* the fucking point of living for crimes upon me and no justice!?

I can't do this anymore, keep having perv's using me and everyone thinks I'm lying. My whole abused life is being judged as a lie. With the sheer lies from the very people who committed these acts, and now the belief of the justice system! There's nothing left. India can't be weighed down with all this. She's settling down nicely with her guy. They look out for each other, and have their own circle of friends, so she won't need me.

My stuff's bad, I'm back, stuck in this vortex of all against me, just like the 1960's again, but this time, I **do** know about suicides.

I can't handle being singled out and pushed from near vindication, to total rejection by the justice system. I refuse to accept in writing, that someone has taken charge of my truth, judged *me* on my childhood, in order to cancel my week of justice. It's shit stirring. It's twisting my lifes' past, to let that filthy, evil bastard walk free. Well it's him or me... and he's lied through what's left of his nicotiny teeth and got away with it all.

Had enough

Attempted Suicide

UNABLE TO DEAL with the shock and anger at the CPS's decision, and not being able to accept their decision delivered to me in writing, I paced around aimlessly throughout the downstairs of my house, talking to myself, asking why I've been completely shat on?, why the lack of justice?... and I repetitively slated dad with all the f's and c's to fit this vile one. I had lost the plot.

No one's to hear my rambling on whilst one second I was seeing household items, the next, me dead in my car.

I grabbed a carrier bag and filled it with tissues, note pad and pen, a bottle of brandy, most of my tablets, then got in my car and drove off. I seemed to be on auto pilot to Lushall, Hampshire to my local garden centre and bought some flexible hose. I went to nearby Tedworth still in Hampshire, not far from my home, and continued on to the supermarket, to grab a sandwich, which I believed once ate, would help make the tablets work quicker *if* I ended up taking them,. Still on autopilot, still cussing and a bit tearful, I found myself heading long into a tank track, until it ended at a set of large metal gates.

I parked up by the gates and sat there for about an hour, then realised the hill I could see up ahead, where I'd just driven from, would have me seen by anyone from there. I drove back down and across the track, and tucked the car into a cutting, covered by tall trees and out of sight of that hill, more importantly me out of view from other people.

The thoughts going on were a diverse range as I sat there staring ahead. There was nothing nice to take my mind off this trail of self- destruction, because the image of me still, and dead in the car, was all that was coming back, which kick started me onto this journey in the first place.

Along with regular gulps of Brandy, I was listening to Simon and Garfunkels' Bridge Over Troubled Water, on my I-pod, half wishing there would be some sort of miracle, like the last verse but no one is going to be 'sailing right behind' to save me from this shite feeling of the abuse, the crap role models of my 'parents', nor the sabotaged education. No one is going to 'Ease my mind' from this lot.

So I kept writing, like I do when i'm stressed. I jotted that last verse along my left forearm, for writings' sake and for later when someone might decide to have that song at my funeral, who knows? I would only find that out once I'm on the other side in spirit.

Between writing, I was still staring ahead at the perimeter of the woodland and going through many thoughts, like 'India's got her partner so she's alright for her future'. Then thinking about the wildlife going on peacefully around me, and then dad, fidgeting in court whilst in the dock, during a pre-trial hearing and I wondered what he said during questioning by the Investigator, and then thought 'It's over' and saw that vision of me by the following morning.

I nipped out for a walk, then whilst up and about, I started to connect the hose to the exhaust pipe, thinking sod it!, it doesn't fit round the outside of the exhaust pipe but I managed to push it tight inside the exhaust pipe instead, then worried about it not being long enough because it'd gone a good way into the exhaust. It reached the back passengers' door. I put the hose through the window, and closed it tight enough to grip the hose, and blocked the surrounding gap with a coat. I got back in the car and done a test run, along with a few more gulps of the brandy. I ran the engine for approximately five minutes, and started feeling the effects of it.

My eyes, nose and lips were stinging, but I was becoming relaxed and still writing and waffling away. I shut the engine off, and waited for nightfall.

It felt right to drift away as it got dark, and be gone by first light.

I'd written about three quarters of an A4 page, mostly to India, and with the song still repeated on my ipod, I felt set to go when darkness falls.

I thought I'd check my phone. I'd had a message from India… "U ok?? Laura called me saying she couldn't get hold of u n now I can't :/". I had four or five missed calls from Unknown, which turned out to be Laura. I had another number for her, and felt I owed her a call, and that would get the news to India.

I texted the other number I had for Laura… "R u still on this fone?". Laura… "Yes. Are you ok?". Me… "No. I'm a bit pissed wiv a hose attached to exhaust…tested & ready t'go.. waitin for th night time.. can't do th tablets bit even tho got thm.

Laura called me, demanding to know where I was. Obviously I didn't want her to know, telling her something like, 'not telling you'. I can't remember all the conversation because I was pretty chilled, pissed, or high on the fumes, and for some reason the calls were being disconnected. She kept calling me back, and to be honest, she was bloody irritating for my head in its state. Then I'd got so pressured by her persistence during this weak moment that felt obligated to tell her I'm on a tank track. "Eliza. Where are you!? You say you're on a tank track, what one, where?!" Suddenly we wasn't connected again, then my mobile was ringing again, and I thought 'Fucks' sake!'

I remember telling her 'it's as you come out of Tedworth, and where you can stick your foot down', I'm sure I said that several times to her. There was more said over about five minutes, including being told to put my keys up on top of the dashboard, which I did.

I dozed off for a moment, then I heard a noise like my washing machine on a spin, I had to see what was happening and saw a police car pulling up at speed, two women Police Constable's got out. One opened my door, and the other one pulled the hose out of the window, and they told me to come out of the car, and sit on the coat on the verge right next to the car.

One of them was chatting to me all the time. I think the other one was on her radio. Then another car pulled up, and Laura got out and crouched down to talk to me. I can't remember now what was said by any of them. There was just too much talking, and I was probably waffling on about being made out to be a liar by the CPS and the courts.

Next to pull up was an ambulance, I had to get in it and the

Paramedics asked questions about my health and done all they had to do. Laura joined me into the ambulance.

I was taken to a Mental Health Team. It felt like everyone there was asking me stuff. There was a room to the right just off of a large foyer, as you entered the building. This room had a bed and tv. I had to go into that room. There was always someone in the room with me, I was on suicide watch.

I briefly chatted with some night staff who were on duty on the locked inner door in the foyer, then laid down on the bed in my room.

Just as I started to settle, I was woken up for an assessment by 3 people. Talk about an 'Alice In Wonderland' moment, everything was surreal. Twenty questions later, after convincing them I'm not going to attempt suicide again, they agreed to let me go home. I was taken home by one of the health team at nearly one am, and they'd arranged for a Police Officer to meet us at my house to give me my keys. At home, I was left with some numbers to call and was told another two health workers will call in the morning, and they'll take me to my car, which spent the night at Tedworth Police Stn.

When the other two health workers turned up the following morning, bearing in mind I felt like shit, it became another surreal feeling during some more questioning. It was all for my benefit to find out about me, to help me, but all I could admit to, was, I don't know what's going on because I keep being asked all the same questions by lots of different people. I can't answer stuff that won't register in my mind. They were concerned about how I was because of what I'd been through and what lead up to the previous nights' behaviour. It was all similar to the previous evenings' questioning and they too gave me contact details, then they drove me to Tedworth Police station and we parted ways.

On the approach to my car, I noticed it had been locked, and because of the locking mechanism and key fob packing up, I had trouble opening it. Well it wasn't going to be straight forward was it, with my recent history.

A Police Officer pulled up and asked me what I'm doing. I told him "I'm trying to collect my car, but couldn't warn whoever drove it here to not lock it". He said, "Is this is your car?". "Yes" I said. "Wasn't you the one taken to the hospital last night?" Me "Uh yeah". He said "They've let you out already?"

Well you can imagine how I felt, being asked by a Police Officer, in a shocked way, about being let out of the psychiatric unit! It was almost comical if I'd been in a better frame of mind. He then said "Wait there a minute please, while I make some checks because I don't think they should've let you out this quick".

I still wasn't feeling 100%, and I don't know if I appeared to be suffering from the after affects but I couldn't have shaped up for anyone He done his checks, and came back to me, and in a well-spoken manner, he said "Eliza, don't let it get that far again. If you start feeling like that again, come here and speak to one of us, nothing is worth doing that for is it". Then he went on to say, "Everyone cares about you". I said "Huh, I dunno about that", with the CPS and dad in mind. He said "Well, you had nearly all the force out looking for you last night, and when we couldn't find you, we came *that* close to getting the helicopter out to look for you".

Totally shocked, I had no idea I'd caused all that. I apologised and thanked him for helping me get in my car, and made my way back across the Plains to home. Even that felt strange, driving home, and past the track, where I was the evening before. I felt a close connection to that place.

That track has since been signed up as "Gate 17".

During the following day, I met India and her partner for a bite to eat. She knew snippets of my previous evening, but not the raw details. She did question my whereabouts because of Laura texting her. She also said, "If you had done anything stupid Mum, it would only be him (dad), who would've won in the end wouldn't it". I told her I knew what she's thinking, "but the consequences aren't as strong as the feelings I had then".

I'd thought everything through, and still felt, what I was doing, was automatically the right decision. There was nothing left for me. I was empty, of love, money, justice, and no one's a real close friend of mine, and as for family, well, the only one left, as I've said, India, who isn't the needy for Mum type, and she's settled with her partner, and we don't live in and out of each-others' houses.

I still went to work on the Monday after all that, and had such a weird feeling, because I never go out to socialise, yet that weekend, I went out, I caused chaos, and no one there in my workroom knew.

I was having flashbacks more often, and wanted to walk out of work, which I did a few times. I was itching to go to dad's place and roll his car over, knock him out, blow his house up, anything to make me feel some kind of payback for the sex abuse he done to me, seeing as the CPS don't know how to recognise a crime when the evidence turns up.

I was advised by one of the Mental Health Team (MHT) to see a counsellor at my GP's surgery and see one of the GP's to get an *official* referral to the MHT. I was able to contact the MHT on a crisis number but really should be referred. You'd have thought I'd be given an automatic referral after attempting suicide wouldn't you.

The counsellor I saw at my GPs' surgery, agreed with a previous 'Pre-court' counsellors' decision that I may well be having symptoms of Post-Traumatic Stress Disorder, because of the sex abuse. She referred me to the MHT to have an assessment for it.

I had met a Doctor as well at my surgery, on a different appointment, who asked me about my thoughts on what I'd done, I told her "I meant to do what I done because of the CPS, and dad. I didn't actually make proper plans to do it, I went out the door carrying anger, at being told my whole life is a lie". She asked, "What about your Daughter, how do you think it would've affected her?" I told her "My Daughter is settled with her partner these days, yes she'd be hurt at first for a while, but probably ok later". She said, "Do you really think she'd get over it?" "At some point afterwards yeah". I added "I still don't see anything wrong with what I done". She said "You don't?" Me, "No, my whole life has been made out to be a lie by a bunch of judgemental people with no idea". This Doctor referred me to the MHT to be assessed for Psychotherapy. She was quite concerned, enough to have called me a couple of times in my lunch breaks after that appointment.

In the meantime, whilst waiting for an appointment to be assessed by the MHT, I'd rang the Crisis Team, (who are the 'out of hours' contacts, from the same MHT) on several of my isolated occasions, because I'd wanted to go back to the tank track because of 'unfinished business' growing stronger which I can only guess is because Laura nipped my suicide attempt in the bud.

The Crisis Team suggested that I distract my thoughts by getting on with anything I am interested in. I was still too bodily knackered for any sort of gardening, swimming or decorating etc, so I started jotting down what was on my mind, trying to make sense of what went on during the build up to, and the evening of the suicide attempt.

I'D WRITTEN;

Sun13/04/14

"I thought I'd be looking back at yesterday, with some sort of shock, selfishness or disbelief at what I'd done, but no, just normality, like when I met India and her partner earlier on. It's as if none of it happened, yet knowing I did do it but without an ounce of surprise at myself'
It wasn't even shocking, like others may have felt about it.
The evenings though, I feel a need to resume my situation, of waiting for darkness, back with the hose connection. Is it because it was nipped in the bud? It's almost annoying now. There's also a feeling of driving off for miles, finding an empty building, like a pill box, near the sea, and locking myself in it, to shut myself away from the world, but have plenty of air, and to hear the sea, nothing else. I'm physically exhausted. I am unable to 'move on' as many people say with ease these days. I can't pull my thoughts away from the need to be back at that place. If I had energy, I'd be there, could hardly drag myself up the stairs, but it's done and I'm hugging my duvet instead".

Mon14/04/14

"Could've cried and walked out of work first thing this morning, it's really difficult to join in conversation. Gradually got a bit better, but I ended up in another room to work for the rest of the day".
Work is my social life in a way, because I don't go out for one reason or another, and usually due to lack of funds. I really had to be at work for distraction, and throw myself back into the norm.
"Later in the evening, I popped 'thank you' notes in to all those involved in the search, the night before last. I still feel like being at the tank track,

and still have that, lock myself away feeling. Something's missing. I'm tired, but that's not why I'm so down, it's because I've been shat on, and I failed to complete on Saturday night. I'm a bit tearful too. Feeling drained, with a headache"... Serves me right, I know.

On Tues 15/04/14 I'd dragged myself through another day, worried with intensity as thoughts of Laura, had suddenly hit me hard. I hadn't seen or thought of her since Saturday evening. What must she be thinking of me? If she is. After everything she's said and done for me, that's how I react! I've not considered how she might've felt, after knowing she's been totally with me, believing what's happened to me, tch, how could I be so thoughtless?

Fri 18/04/14

"I tried to start everything as a normal day. I'm not at work today. I popped out early, to get paint for a Revell model Chinook helicopter I'm making. I challenged myself to a bit of digging in the back garden. Whilst out there, I was getting images of dad, and of Laura chatting with the Police. I wondered what must've gone through her mind.

On a break from digging, I looked up CPS website, and soon realised I shouldn't have. It wasn't long before I started feeling annoyed and upset at seeing a 'celebrate' page, at the successful conclusions to recent court cases, which they'd previously decided there was enough evidence for etc. I was surprised to not see pages for 'Our Pathetic Decisions' on there. That would've used up most of their website.

It feels like a Saturday, have a need to be back there at the track again, but not in the possessed sense that I had last weekend.

When I went there to carry out the suicide, I'd already done it in my minds' eye. I saw myself dead in the car whilst buying the hose on the way, and driving to wherever it felt right to stop.

I'm really trying to plan forward now though. The garden, hanging baskets, wall paint, chinook paint etc..

I've left a message with the Police, to let Laura, know, I want to do the Victims' Right To Review, because I've disagreed with the CPS's decision.

SAT 19/04/14

Laura and her boss came to my house to chat, and give me the letter, which I couldn't accept last week. It has the information on it about disagreeing with CPS's decision. I didn't really know what to say, I wanted to give Laura a hug, but would it have been wrong and against protocol? I had previously added my praises for Laura when I was on the phone to the Police yesterday. I should've said it all again to her, but I didn't know what to say. I had already written half of my complaint to the CPS, which Laura and her boss read. When they left, I felt pretty low and tearful, for a 'final' feeling. I cracked on with the rest of my complaint and felt a tad better for writing it out.

The following, is the letter in reply to the CPS's letter of 03/04/14.

I do understand what you mean when you came to your decision to stop the trial.

I also understand you need to find a balance. "Being fair and being seen to be fair are the cornerstones of everything we do".

Can you explain to me, just how you see it as being 'fair' to me then please?

I was sexually abused by my 'father', from the age of 5 or 6, until the age of approximately 15.

When I was 13, (1972/3) I was raped by my friends' Brother.

I reported the rape for the record in approximately 1997 because my late Mum hadn't done anything about it after I'd blurted it out to her after it happened, and I felt a need to get it recorded, which was done at a South London Police Station.

I reported it again to get something done about it in 2006/7, at the same station, because it was affecting me badly, once my Daughter turned 13.

During the phone calls, and a home visit, the investigating Officer in Kent asked lots of questions, made one suggestive remark, and basically got nowhere…

I told him I thought I'd seen one of the witnesses some months back, but guessed it might've been a dream…

Talking about dreams had been relevant to that report because nightmares and flash backs were happening again about the rape and the abuse, for which I was having counselling in Ramsgate, Kent.

I only found out about the investigating Officer including 'might've been a dream' in his investigation notes, in the letter of your decision, when I also learned he'd also added It 'maybe untrue' and have since made a complaint to the Met Police about this.

If I have managed to explain it in that clear and simple fashion, I'm sure I can put the defendant straight, give just as much or more back AND keep any Jury clear on the facts, which are the truth.

I am not a liar. I wouldn't have the memory or the mental energy to hold on to this lot if they were lies. Furthermore, I don't go to the Police, and report every dream/nightmare I have about my 'father'/abuser attempting to shaft me, or lying next to me with a boner!…

I didn't dream about being raped when I was 13. I was definitely, well and truly raped after I was pulled through a bedroom door, in front of some friends, who were pushed away from that door…

I can't accept the way someone in the CPS has quickly and thoughtlessly judged me, because they've grabbed a snippet of that shoddy and wrongful rape report… Robbing me of my chance of justice against my sex abuser, who robbed me of my whole childhood.

This pathetic, non-relevant decision, shell shocked me to say the least, sending me to attempt to take my life last Saturday.

I'm 53, honest, and doing my best.

The defendant can throw anything they want at me, they can exaggerate, sing, dance and lie until they're blue in the face, but they won't stop the Jury, from focusing on the 10 or so years of sex abuse that I suffered, because I won't let them.

From what I can gather also, he (that abuser) just about corroborated with my statement anyway.

I see on the CPS website, that you don't reinstate the trials on 'Victims' Right to a Review', when you've made a wrong decision. Isn't that biased then, by not reinstating the trial? because the way I see it, it is a wrong decision, it's not going to allow the trial to be reinstated, I'm robbed of justice because of that, which looks pretty much biased in favour of the abuser.

Why end the proceedings of a trial, before the innocent victim gets the chance to have the review, or appeal?.. Again, this is totally being biased, and feels heavily judgemental to me, the victim.

I don't see any fairness whatsoever in cutting a trial, before you've thoroughly investigated what you've based your decision on, and before I got the chance to put the truth to you.

That's not protecting the innocent. It's ripping justice out from under my feet, and rubbing my nose in it.

How many successful suicides, linked with CPS's decision making, has there been since setting up?

Can you reduce it by one and let my trial be reinstated now please?

I have just received your letter.

In the paragraph that starts 'The new information'. The time delay, of enquiring about the allegation, was because I'd done it for the record initially, and like I said earlier, it was affecting me when my Daughter became 13...... I could've said that to the defendant.

Also, I wasn't told that the witnesses contradicted my account. If they've found a contradiction to my account, then they must've remembered the incident...... I could've said that to the defendant too.

The 'May have been a dream' bit has been explained earlier.

The following paragraph 'We are also aware'. Referring to an allegation of rape I made against my friend of my brother? Well, the defendant is more than welcome to try that against me but I've never said that, because it never happened. It's a mistake in someone's reading or writing of it.

The rape, which I have mentioned throughout all this, is about my friends' brother, the same rape that had other friends of mine being a witness to, back in the 'The new information' paragraph. I could've said that to the defendant.

It could've been cleared up when the defendant would've chose to chuck that one at me, which would've 'clearly undermined the defendant', leaving them scrambling to throw the Jury off the truth. So there's nothing for them to adduce, apart from the one rape I've reported.....Which the defendant could bring on.

The Code of Practice for Victims of Crime... I don't seem to fit into any of the categories there... I know there's lots to read there, but what I did look through, doesn't have Adult victims of child abuse.

Knowing my abuser, once he's questioned for a while, he would've slipped up with the lies he's told, and the Jury would've heard that, had you given the chance for it to proceed.

Disappointed with the decision that has been reached? Yes, I thought that, whilst I had the hose connected to the exhaust pipe last Saturday evening, waiting for it to get dark. (My investigating Officer got the Police to find me before it got dark).

Seeing as there's been a mistake, exactly at the point you made your decision on, can the decision be reversed? I know it states it only reverts to an apology, but my trial was stopped purely because it would undermine me as a witness, but that was based on a written mistake, which wasn't part of the case because it didn't happen.

Miss Eliza I Fynn

Ps… I will be contacting ** on Tuesday 22nd.

Mental Health

AFTER THE SUICIDE attempt at Gate 17 in Tedworth I started seeing a Psychologist.

Ha haa! If only it was *that* straightforward.

- April and May 2014 and before the trial date, I'd had two or three sessions of counselling at my GP's' surgery for the yet to be diagnosed PTSD. My counsellor was about to refer me to Wiltshire mental health team (MHT) for an assessment to see if it is PTSD I have, and to see another Counsellor or Psychologist within the MHT. So I'd joined the queue into the MHT.
- April 2014… The Crown Prosecution Service did their bit to send me suicidal, for which I got sectioned for half the night at Wiltshire MHT, where I was assessed by three psychologist/ counsellor people, to see if I was safe to go home, and yes, I was fine to leave the building and taken home by a night Health Worker.
- May 2014… I was given an appointment to see someone 'M' in the MHT. This was since and because of the suicide attempt, and not because of the referral by the GP's counsellor. Even though the counsellor at my GP's surgery done a referral to MHT, I was advised by the MHT, to go back through the GP, to get a referral back to the MHT before getting to see any Counsellor or Psychologist. Straight away and in the meantime, I leant heavily on M for help, often on the phone to her several

times during my walk outs from work and flashbacks prior to and during those walkouts. I nearly talked her ears off… and she always helped me.

- June 2014… I was referred to the MHT, and started seeing E, a Community Psychiatric Nurse, (CPN) who, just like M, allowed me to be autonomous, yet they were concerned about my next moves. Even I didn't know what I'd do next. My moods were mostly dictated by my nightmares and flashbacks, and the need to wring someone's neck in the CPS, and murder my dad. So M, and more often now E, were hit with new shite scenarios from me, and me leaving a cliff hanger of whether I'd be arrested for anything from harassment to point blank murder. That was my mind frame all the time. I imagine I bored or worried the pants off people with it. If I'd got justice, my mind frame would've been completely different. If I hadn't been abused, I'd be a better person, but I wouldn't have met these lovely empathic people at Wiltshire MHT.
- July 2014… I got a referral to see T, my Psychologist, to start on 05.August.2014, sharing the alternate weeks with him and E, and chucked in the odd review with Consultant Psychiatrist-Dr S, along with T and E.

So that was from the 12.April.2014 to 05.August.2014, before I managed to have help for my psychological state. Five months after the suicide attempt.

M and E during this wait, totally held space for the damaged mentality of mine.

Personally though, on the night I was sectioned, I needed to have slept it off, then on waking, seen M, E or T, straight away. I really needed these guys, to hear me in the next hours, prescribe immediate medication, and for us to learn what went on in my head during the build up to the hose-exhaust moment.

The impact the CPS and dads' sex abuse/lies had on me, happened then. The suicide attempt was my first voice since the cancelled trial. I was still within that shock-like experience, needing help right there. Five months later, diluted it, and made it harder to explain the scale of this impact. It also gave me more time to re visit the suicide attempt place several times, and to think about doing it again.

It felt irritatingly dragged out, waiting for referral #one, to the MHT, then repeat that referral, request #two, then referral to E, #three, then wait for another referral this time to T #four. Yes it all helped, but my rocky, lost moment was five months before.

So, back to chatting with E, I was attending a couple of weekly sessions of talking with E. Initially, our meet ups were more like an ongoing assessment, so that she could give a report to the Consultant Psychiatrist, who then assessed me, with her and another counsellor, and decided together, who I should see for psychology.

I didn't hold back on what had to be said either. It was good to say exactly what was making me feel aggressive and stressed one moment, then what had me feeling completely sunk in the next.

I still even now (July '16) feel pretty much the same about revenge as if I hadn't had any tablets, but I guess these tablets have slightly mellowed me out of physically seeking revenge. Maybe it's the weight gain they cause, which makes me too lumpy and tired, to bother getting revenge on nonce dad.

When it finally started, I would see T my Psychologist weekly, and still with E on a weekly basis, then gradually, as my suicidal tendencies crept away, and *didn't* rush back out of the blue, I saw them fortnightly.

It was my time to chat about anything, when seeing E, and in turn she offered some wise words. This woman is sound and sincere. She made every effort to get to me when I couldn't get to the mental health clinics in Wiltshire, which was the case for most of our meet ups, because I'd been banned from driving for three months because of the suicide attempt. It was important to keep my appointments with E, and because of that, she either came to my home, or we sat in her car outside my works during my lunch hour. She knew I done a lot of writing, and she'd read most of what I wrote, which was often a release of my anger, and then I'd check it through again, and delete the bulk of swearing. She didn't just do this chat, she covers a variety of Mental Health departments. She also reported back to my Consultant Psychiatrist about the tablets she had put me on for the PTSD and depression, and what affect they have on me, why she's changed them, and my progress etc. The tablets did not affect my driving, when I *was* allowed to drive.

A quick brief about my driving ban… Way back in November 2013, my driving licence was already with the dvla for updating for a new job, but it was taking months to process, so I contacted them to leave it because I was meant to start the job in February 2014, and this was now April 2014. There was no longer a reason to update it because they'd taken so long, the job had gone. I contacted them to leave it as it was, and return my driving licence to me.

They only had *one* job to do! Just bung it in an envelope, and send it back to me. (Ok, two jobs). They couldn't just do that. Oh of course they bloody couldn't!

Everything was fine before. Just *send* it back. Nope! Returning it to me meant they had to make further medical checks. What the hell for!? It was absolutely fine before, back in the November. Nothing had changed. They revoked my licence for 3 months because of the "Psychiatric Illness"…Wonderful, I mean, really helpful!

So, this was one of my angry rants to E, who also found this crap I was being dealt, total bonkers. She took the dvla departments' contact details, and sorted it out with my Consultant Psychiatrist, who in turn wrote a very good letter to the dvla, assuring them I was capable of driving and need to drive for my job and my therapy with T which in itself was "an important part of her psychological recovery". Thank you Dr S.

Dvla, decided to let me drive again. No, this wasn't as straightforward as it reads either! I wish I was joking, but no. I had to re-apply for my own, same driving licence.

So, with another tonne of paperwork filled in, and other signatures etc. Oh plus an updated photograph too, it was all sent to them. I did get my licence back, but it was only for a year. Why? It wasn't like the ban was still standing. No reason… Maybe the dvla was thinking, "We just like to piss you off while you're down". Well, I eventually got the proper licence, only until 2018 though. "It's October 2018, Ive re-applied for my licence again. They've sent me a questionnaire about my C-PTSD. I completed it and sent it back straight away. They replied telling me they need to write to my Doctor… This is where it's left at."

Well, back to E, where I would say all sorts to her, from my anger, lack of trust, flashbacks, medication, walk outs from work, to those problems with dvla, and things I said to T, and then rant off what I thought about my so called brothers, and slagging them and nonce dad off. Nothing I said shocked this woman, and she often suggested better ideas to help me escape my near delirium.

T, who blushed and grinned every time I swore, and made me laugh, during the sessions when I refused to call 'dad', 'dad', for reasons we now know. So in turn, T totally respected me by calling him "shitface" as well, thank you T. That was funny though, hearing a swear word from him.

The first 4 or 5 sessions, were about my basic family history and all the failed relationships etc. We did touch on the sex abuse. It'll never leave my mind, but I was going to be working on dealing with the impact, which the cancelled trial had on me and the affect that the sex abuse and dad's lies had on me, and he was thinking about possibly having me try EMDR. Eye Movement Desensitizing Reprocessing… He'd only choose for me to go into it if the Psychology doesn't completely help.

I didn't end up having the EMDR. I can't fully remember the full scale of the work we did, so I'm working on the summary letter from T, and filling in anything I remember around it.

"We identified a number of specific areas of difficulty which you needed help with, including the impact of the CPS's decision not to allow the trial to go ahead against dad, and the associated feelings of anger and at times hopelessness about it. We also identified longer standing feelings of insecurity and trust issues in relationships and reactivated experiences (flashbacks) from childhood sex abuse/trauma.

We spent quite a lot of time thinking and dealing with the emotional fallout that you was experiencing in relation to the CPS's decision. During the meetings"

I did express my sheer anger about it.

T "and then expressed the need for revenge".

I admit I was hopeless about this sex abuse upon me, gone by without justice for it, and that my nonce smirking at me across the court, which created a need to wipe his face off his head.

T "When feeling very angry and revengeful, at times you have felt a strong pull to express this via social media and taken actions yourself, which have led to you being arrested and cautioned by the Police. During our sessions, I have wanted to validate your feelings about what happened to you as a child and in relation to the CPS, whilst also strongly encouraging you to make more positive choices about progressing your life and trying to find lawful and legitimate ways of expressing your unhappiness about the decision of the CPS. More recently, you have attended a demonstration in London, which you spoke at and also made contact with a sympathetic MP and I hope these channels provide some support and validation for your concerns.

We have reflected on how you become very preoccupied with your father, and the associated anger has at times led you to making choices, which I have described as more self-destructive and have taken you further away from creating the life that you might want or value for yourself. We have also discussed how it is likely in the future that difficult feelings will show up at times and when feeling angry and distressed, it will be very important for you to respond to yourself with greater care and self-compassion and try to just notice the pull towards self-destructive behaviours, but not act on them. The exercises we did in relation to staying present and grounding skills, including Mindfulness, might be helpful when feeling a strong pull towards more self-destructive behaviours.

We have also talked about trying to build the life that you want for yourself and you have expressed an interest in a number of things that you would like to work towards in the future, whilst also recognising that it is financially challenging for you at this time, given that your work has now ended. I am also aware that you have been writing about your experiences and that being able to express yourself through your writing has been very important to you. At our last session, we spoke briefly about possible options for self-publishing, something that you would like to do in the future.

Clearly, trust issues, as previously mentioned and associated feelings of insecurity will continue to be challenging for you in the future and are more likely to show-up in intimate relationships. However, hopefully you can find someone who you feel close to and safe with, in the context of a secure relationship. I think that past memories of abuse which show up when being more physically intimate can be worked through and resolved over time."

All true. However, as we know, nothing will rid my head of the abuse and flashbacks.

So, I keep taking the tablets… experience occasional bruxism, angry thoughts and weight gain…

I occasionally use social media to rant off about the lenient, pathetic sentences given to nonces, or the daft, slap on the wrist, walk from court, dirty, vile wimps, caught downloading category A or less, photographic images of baby and child rape, which *does* ruin their small lives. I don't as often now slag each one off that has been caught, ruining babies' and childrens' lives.

I've done stacks of slagging off for across 2014, 15 and 16. Sure I still feel the same anger. I'd like to round them all up and just sit there with a gatling gun, swinging left to right down the depths of rows, of the many, dirty, evil bastards, but where's it getting us? What will it do to help those already ruined little lives? Any amount of anger on social media or face to face with nonces, is all too little too late. Those little lives are already ruined by the selfish, vile lowlife perverts. Like my dad

There's a guy I know of, who's actually stopping potential paedophiles acting out their evil upon children and babies. He sets up decoys online, arranges to meet the paedophiles, catches them out on a sting then he sees they're prosecuted. Then his hard work is almost undone again when the paedophiles are given lenient, pathetic sentences. That's if they haven't walked free from court.

There are more groups doing decoys nowadays. The Police work hard too, towards prevention of sex crimes, but rarely do we hear about nonces being caught sniffing round children, *before* they ruin childrens' lives. Rarely do we read about paedophile rings being caught, and those nonces given over one hundred years each in jail, like the States give during sentencing.

There are hundreds, most likely thousands of little lives ruined before they've properly begun, at the hands of the perverts. My heart goes out to the other victims and their families involved.

T was very patient with me, during my rant offs and often had to gently remind me to get back to the subject of the impact the abuse and cancelled trial had on me.

CAUTIONED.

After the decision from the Crown Prosecution Service's review, and having their door slammed in my face, which lead me to attempting suicide. I was unable to rid myself of an obsessive and savage anger. I wanted dad dead.

Why should I take all that abuse, to then hear him lying through his teeth, then be forced to accept that they all see me as a liar!? Since this began, I've always said it's going to be him or me by the end of this justice stuff.

Well, *I'd* already attempted suicide because of it. *I've* already served my mental life sentence, so whatever happens next, is less. This revenge feeling was consuming, it's much stronger than the consequences I could face.

Headstrong I was, I'd be thinking every hour, day and night, about what act of revenge I would do. This was all I was for the first eighteen months after the trial was cancelled. I told E my CPN, that I'm right up there with anger, I wanted justice and him in prison, I can't have that, so the next best thing is revenge, it needs to be done.

Planning revenge was what actually got me to sleep some nights, but other nights, I'd be so angry, I was never getting to sleep. My heart would be racing, and I would jump out of bed about three a.m, into some clothes, and sneak out to my car as quietly as possible. I'd start the car and go, all in the same move, and drive to his house. I'd do a recc'e of the surroundings of his house, checking for cameras etc.

All was dark apart from the headlights of my car and the dull yellow lamp post lights.

The security camera a few yards from the main entrance, wouldn't have got my number plate on entering the area he lives in, but could've got it on my exit from there. I knew I had to be careful about this. I tested it out, to see whether I'd be caught and reported. I put some garden items in different places round his parking lot. I was fairly smug with myself as got back into my car and drove home. I slept very well with a smile on my face after that.

As trivial as this small action was, it was worth it to me. It was the fact that I was there, and at three thirty am, whilst he was asleep, and I wasn't stifling my mind with images of dad wanting my body. Also, it was the fact that dad had no power over me. I had power over him. His control was non-existent, whilst I was there, when he had no knowledge of it. What a difference to my state of mind, especially the next morning, when I was near euphoric!

I had no Police on my doorstep from this…not this incident anyway.

Some other nights were almost the last straw. One night, I'd woken from having a nightmare about him following me, brushing his hand across the crotch of his trousers with an erection.

All I could think was, get another bike, I'm an ex motorcyclist, mainly owned road bikes up to and including 750's, but I thought about getting a black trail bike and wait until he's coming back from town, and do a drive by shooting. If I got a small dark, and fast bike, it would be less easy to see if on camera, and find when I dump it somewhere. The hardest bit would've been purchasing the gun.

The best idea yet, was that. It fits exactly into my mood with good balance, and yes I even bullet pointed it in my plan… coincidentally.

- I'm sat next to dad's car. I'm on my bike at traffic lights during a dark evening, which would mirror us next to each other in the bathroom, settee and beds.
- I make him look at me, and see the gun, like dad made me notice his erection on the settee, and again the bathroom and beds.
- I aim the gun, which mirrors dad's approach to my body.
- Aimed, so that the bullet goes through both jaw hinges.
- Trigger pulled. Dad's' penis forced onto and into me.
- Now *dad's* the defenceless one and without a voice, which mirrors my childhood.
- Trigger pulled again. This time, in dad's' bollocks, as a preventative measure to ensure he ruins no other lives, and again, mirrors dad trying forcefully to rape me on the settee, which fuckin' hurt, whilst *I* was defenceless without a voice… until this book.
- I go to sleep my own Hero

I then planned to empty my house, and ride or drive off out of sight, but then what? Hide from my nonce, should he remain alive? Hide from the Police, for the rest of mine and/or dad's' lives, whilst they're protecting him?

That was the main idea to get me to sleep, and had money been no object then, I saw me actually doing that. I had nothing to lose except maybe a house and garden. Prison was nothing to worry about, apart from the claustrophobic side of it. I'd still see my India.

Remember, I suffered sex abuse all of my childhood, I sought justice, justice, which I was getting until it slammed doors on me even with those charges still standing. Dad starts to act like he's innocent. Dad *knows he's guilty*. The Police and I know he's guilty. Dad gets let off. Wrong.

My other plan, which I stupidly blurted out to someone, during the excitement of it manifesting, they in turn informed the Police, was to roll his car on its' side and write 'BANKSY' across it. I got as far as searching for longer ratchet straps than I already owned, and car jacks, so that I could part lift it up and pull it with my car and straps, bearing in mind I'm alone doing all that, but blurting it out, instantly put the mockers on that plan, but it helped me sleep when planning it out.

Maybe I'll just have to wait and see what Karma does.

It wasn't enough, to suffer those nightmares of dad, which forced me awake, just to lay there planning again, whilst all that time, dad's been happily asleep with no disturbances like I still suffer. So I started writing my anger down again, like many years ago.

It's still not enough to match my anger though. I'm the one awake, not him! He's the one who forced me awake. If I can't sleep, then neither the hell can he!

I purchased the cheapest mobile phone. I done a few calls to my mobile from the new phone, obviously blocking my number before dialling, just to make sure my new phone wouldn't be traced. The next bad dream I had triggered by him, I rang his number.

It was three fifteen a.m. The line was connected, the phone was ringing…and ringing…and ringing. It stopped. I heard a very out of breath voice struggle to say 'Hello'. I went to disconnect the call, and it wouldn't work. 'Hello' he said again. I was tensing up, trying to not giggle under my breath in case he heard me. I had to shut the phone down completely, but still worried in case he heard me, I switched it back on again, deleted the call log, and able to breathe again. It was a bit scarey but felt 'Yeah', 'good'. Now I can sleep…until the next time.

My writing was still increasing with the shock and anger. My CPN was totally understanding of me. She said you will be the first person the police will come to, if you sought revenge on him and he'll be having you in court, and you'll be the one being prosecuted, then you'll look like the trouble maker. I knew what she meant. I said, "Even if I ended up in prison, for murdering the cunt, I'd still wake up every morning with a fat smile on my face". She told me I won't. That was probably the only agree to disagree moment we had during all the tireless support she gave me.

E also said "Eliza, you like writing. It's stopped you going back to attempt suicide and actual revenge. Keep on writing, because if you did continue to write a book about it, it would be the best revenge you could ever get on him. So, Thank you E. I continue to write and increase it to keep up with the changes that happen surrounding the abuse, justice system and mental health as the months go by.

There was several more three am nightmares, sneak outs and recce's gone on. He was none the wiser, he didn't notice anything I'd moved around. Well, he may've noticed but I didn't get any come back from it. There were also several more phone calls and hang ups on the exhausted 'hello"s. and me sleeping like a log afterwards.

To add to the phone calls and recce's, I'd been so angry that my writing became letters or notes to him. This one below is the first bout of angry writing he got from me.

MEMORY JOGGED YET!?

I'd sent photo's and put the addresses of where dad abused me, but I wasn't able to include them in this book for legal reasons. I had put North London and what happened there, then put South London and what happened there, then put Kent and what happened to me there and included photographs of the houses, flats and me, then wrote all the vile details.

It was good getting that lot off my mind, and even better knowing he read it the following morning. A true statement, received by the guilty one, lead to me having the police call to ask me about it, and advising me/warning me to not send anything else or contact him in any other way.

Yeah right! That's less, stacks less than what I've been through from him and the CPS' s' decision.

With a few more three a.m phone calls behind me, my anger wrote the next written piece;

My swearing does seem to also be my anger management. I seem to feel a tad better after it.

Round two:

"Dear Cunt!

You must be feeling pretty smug with yourself by now, with the Crown Prosecution Service deciding to stop the trial, of 12 charges against you, of perving on me.

You was 33 when you started forcing me to have sex with you.

It carried on and on, it started when I was around 5, at the flat, but I also remember when I was about 2 or 3, in London, when you forced me onto mum's' breast while you was wanking yourself off!

Back to the flat. That lot just went on and on didn't it, you filthy fuckin' bastard!

All those bath times on Sundays. There I was, an innocent 5 year old in the bath. It *was* normal, when I could play with the dog bubble bath, then you had to come in there to 'make sure i'm washing properly'. But you didn't did you. Infact, you was the very person who changed it all for the worse for me.

You just couldn't keep it clean could you. Remember this; "Put ye arms forward like dis for daddy, make it like titties like ye mammy". and "Hold dis, hold it really tight, that's right, now don't tell anybody d'ye hear? This is daddy and Elizas' secret, don't even tell ye mammy". and "Right, that's it, now move it back and forwards or up and down like dis". That's when you grabbed my hand and held it on there tighter and forcing me to wank you off. Yes it IS true. I remember you entering the bathroom, asking me "Do ye wanna play daddys' little game?" I remember nodding 'no'. Then you turned the light off, then you'd say "Hold dis for daddy". When it was all over and done with, you'd wash/wipe my hands and body of the semen all over me, even then you'd stroke my vagina and make that stupid fuckin' noise!

It didn't stop there did it, I mean, that must've been what I was fuckin' born for wasn't it-your sexual satisfaction-One almighty sick fucker you!

Onto the living room next, Oh! Or was it the bedroom-yours of course. No i'll move into the living room. I wanted to play wrestling, which you never let me play when you played it with my 'brothers' (yeah, question that one) but back to me and you. You had dark trousers with I think button through fly. You allowed me to play wrestling with you on the settee. I asked you "What's that?" It was your cock, erect, you had no pants on. That's when you told me what it was and what it's for, correction, showed me. I was sat with my back to one end of the settee and facing you. You told me to shove down, which I innocently did.

You pushed yourself onto me, and pushed your penis onto my vagina, hard. You actually attempted to rape me, whilst feeding me with your bullshit about "Mammy & daddy" crap. It's crap because you two were certainly no role model of 'parents' and crap again because it's all you ever lectured to me, and you know what? You're one hell of a cunt, for the attempted rape of you so called 'daughter' aged 5!

Far from finishing, that didn't finish there did it. Whether it was the same game and day or not, I don't fuckin' give a shit, but 'wrestling' again, you was blowing raspberries on my legs, inner thighs and groin then went onto licking my vagina within the same raspberry blowing. For that, you are the most rancid excuse of a human being I've ever set eyes on.

Now the bedroom, yours and 'mum's, wherever she was all those nights & days. I never forget it, that stench of ash from those ashtrays each side of your bed, the nicotiny pillows, me laying beside you, to your left. You had your back to me. I think this was the first night of many. I rested my arm over you, as an innocent hug. You turned round asked me if it's "this" I wanted, your erect penis again, accompanied by the stench of your nicotiny breath. There it all happened again didn't it. 5, 6 & 7 yrs old and wanked you off in bed again and again, semen wiped off with a spat on, nicotine handkerchief you dirty fuckin' piece of scum!

Rose's flat-I had to go over there because you was shaggin' her behind mums' back, so while she (mum) was away, we had tea there after school. I would get asked by you or her or just told to go home over to mums' flat. One day I was over Rose's when we were all in the kitchen, you told her I was tired, cos I was clearly confused about my mums' whereabouts and questioning yous, with mouth trembling etc. Being told i'm tired meant you had to take me to bed, Rose's bed. She went into the living room, you stayed in the bedroom... Unfuckin' believable, you got me sexually satisfying you with a hand job yet again!

Never mind the fact that Rose was there in the other room, or was you hoping to get caught and have her join in huh?!

Never mind that my head was full of worry that my mum wasn't there anymore and I was completely lost and stressed out about it! You selfish, perverted, shitfaced cunt!

So it all continued in your house didn't it. After leaving us for Rose, having another daughter, turning the knife in mums' back evermore with your self centered way. You got me visiting you's there. I was in my teens at the time, your filthy habits, you tried to continue, by grabbing my breasts and commenting to Rose about how big and firm they are, as if i'd not had any thoughts of feelings about it. Yes Eliza, the big lump of putty and one who can be manipulated most easily by her 'father'.

Remember sending me upstairs to your dressing table for something, which wasn't in that drawer? But the thing easily visible was a vibrator, and you came up there, and looked at me as if to say, 'd'you want to play with this? That's when I said 'well I can't find it' and walked off.

You just never fuckin' stopped did you! You should've been locked up fuckin' years ago. By the way, how is M**** F***** doing?...You got closer to her too?

You're so fuckin' selfish, still getting your chances with me at South London house before running away to Carlisle! Never once asking how I actually was, even these later years, you gutlessly tell the others in the /your family that "Oh she's in one of her not talking moods again!"

'She'-just another person of the opposite sex, and has no upbringing of love, emotions or self respect.

Him...He; you-Lack of respect towards own flesh and blood!

Happy to ridicule members of own flesh and blood anywhere, anytime in front of strangers too!

Selfish to the core, particularly when needing to satisfy sexual needs, and uses own flesh and blood for satisfaction.

Youngest brother knows what went on in the bathroom – remember him banging on the bathroom door when I was in the bath, giving you a hand job!? Funny how he chose to **not** remember that when doing a police statement, yet he remembered it when I mentioned it in 2009... Where there's a will, there's a way huh!?

I was raped when I was 13, you was groping my breasts from them days at least until I was 15, anytime I saw you!

You're full of yourself, self- righteous, self centered and right fuckin' up yourself!

You're perverted to the fuckin' hilt!.. and I'm never, fuckin' ever, going to give up getting justice done for myself!

By the time I've finished with this search for your other victims and my justice, you'll be wishing yourself more than 6ft under.

My next life is going to be a million miles away from cunts like you.

You and all the other perverts can rot the fuck in hell!

Do y'self a favour, go hand y'self in to the Police, before someone else has to take you to do it!"

Well that went down well... Dad had the cheek to give it to the Police again, trying to make out he's innocent.

A week or so later, the Police arrived at the door basically asking me if I wrote the letter. I admitted it because after all, it says the truth and nothing but all over it. The Police totally understood the reason behind my poking my angry letters through his door during the night. They also warned me I could be done for harassment if I kept this up...

I was asked if I'd approached him in the local town..

I was avoiding his town since all this began, to avoid seeing dad. I'm not scared of him. I was just weary of my anger at him if I saw him, and how far would go with it, especially in public. I always wanted to tell him to grow some and own up to what he done to me. (I haven't strayed from the caution bit, still building up to it).

If I had a lift to and from work, sometimes my friend who was driving, would need to stop in the shop in the town, and always said "You're fine, you won't bump into him here".. I used to say, "What, do you know something I don't know?" Months of this, and chancing it with India driving us there couple of times.

On the 29.11.14, India was driving us to the stores for a bit of Christmas shopping, and decided on dads' local town. I told her I'd sit in the car whilst she grabbed some shopping then. She said "He won't be here mum". I said "How do you and (car sharer) seem to know he won't be here?" and "Has he snuffed it and no one's telling me, or something?" India said "Come on".

We'd gone up and down a couple of aisles of the car park checking it out making sure his car wasn't there. I looked out for a bent aerial he had on his car, which I'd noticed when doing a recce at his house before. I couldn't see any of his make of car, with a bent aerial, so I chanced it.

Walking towards the store, bruxism full on. (teeth bitten together hard).

We were just across the drive from the main doors and cashpoints, and India said "Oh no mum, he's there at the cashpoint", I looked at her to see where she was absolutely glaring hard. It was the perpetrator himself. "Ah right, un-finished business!" I said. I only had a few paces to go to be next to him, so was racking my brains of all that I planned to say to him, and in the right order.

India grabbed my arm to attempt to stop me walking further, bless her. "No mum, don't go over there, don't do anything". She didn't know whether I was going to lay into him or scream at him or what I was going to do.

He was at the left of the two cashpoints. So I went to the right one and leant against it, and said to him "When are you gunna grow some balls and admit what you done to me huh?" He glanced at me, then looked away to what he was doing, rolling his tongue under his upper lip, and not a word said. I expected him to tell me to 'fuck off', but he just totally ignored me after looking as if he didn't know me, so I said, "What, haven't you got anything to say then?"

He finished at the cashpoint, and walked into the foyer. I thought, 'shit', he's going in the store', then I realised, he's cutting right through the foyer to leave. I said "Oh, hard of hearing now is it? Selective hearing, cos you know your guilty!"

India asked if I was alright, I told her "I can't believe he looked at me as if I've never been anything to do with him, what a cunt!" I was shaking with adrenalin and anger. India told me what made her notice him there, which was really funny, and brought a laugh out of us about it.

Seriously though, something's got to change for the better for me. The CPS should reopen the trial or better still, just stop ripping justice out from under victims' feet. Or dad should admit to the Police what he's done to me.

Every time I think of him slating me to the rest of that so called family, yet knowing full well what he done to me across the years, makes me want to make a scene at his place, and get the word spread around about his perving on me years. Lets' hope this book continues to spread the truth around.

So in answer to the Police Constables' question, did I approach my perpetrator? Yes, sure did.

Back to my revenge letters and phone calls.

I kept it up. It's still stacks less than what I'd been put through, so I wrote another one;

11.APRIL.2015

"How do you sleep at night? After what you done to me all through my destroyed, sabotaged childhood and education, do you not feel an ounce of guilt?

I had hoped you'd man up, and admit to what you done to me, but no, you just sit there, thinking how lucky you've been to believe you've got off scot free.

You're a filthy, disgusting perv, and that for sure is one thing you, I and any other victim of yours, will never be free of.

One year ago, I attempted suicide, because of what you done to me, then made me out to be a fucking liar. You, sexually abused and attempted to rape me when I was 5 or 6 years old, and while I try dealing with it and getting justice for it, you make my life, all my sabotaged childhood, out to be one fuckin' huge lie!

When all along, you are the fuckin' gutless, lying bastard! You know damn well what you done to me!

Did it make you feel more of a man then, whilst you was 33 and I was 5 and you was on top of me on the settee in our flat?!

Does it make you feel innocent, once you've called the Police on me? How long does it take you to pluck up courage to look them in the eye ay!?

Are you, or was you raping babies aswell? How many other young girls did you have?

Don't think you can call the Police, and decide you're innocent, then think you can forget it. I've lived with the stench of your body odour, and tobacco breath all my life, and as long as it takes, you for sure, are going to live with it until you man up and admit what you done, or until you drop fuckin' dead!

If you don't like this truth in writing, admit <u>all</u> that you done to me next time you call the Police. Tell them what <u>you</u> done, and caused to your own flesh & blood! If my letters are pissing you off, what the fuck do you think I'm going through, to need to write the fuckers!? This is never over!

You're a lying, deceitful, gutless, dirty, cunting liar!"

So, another colourful letter went to dad, leaving me temporarily feeling quite cool with myself. I don't know how he has the cheek to actually tell the Police. Would he dare contact them and report me yet again?

Yep.

I was tidying up the weeds under the hedge in my front garden, sat down there, also chatting with a neighbour. A Police car pulled up in the next door neighbours' parking bay. I genuinely thought nothing of it, and long forgotten about my three am postal service to shitface.

The first Police Constable to talk asked if I'm Eliza Fynn I said "Yeah?" I checked that this isn't to do with my Daughter, and that she's alright. It wasn't about India. I said to my neighbour, "Ah that'll be for me then", and went indoors with them. I was informed they'd had a complaint from shitface. Well they told me his birth name. I said "What, again? You should arrest him for keeping on complaining about his victim of his sex abuse etc".

They offered to take me to the Police station.

Actually they told me they're arresting me for "Harassment of an old man…in fear of violence". Ha haa! How the truth hurts ay! I was fine about it, in fact, I felt a bit good for pissing my perpetrator off!

I was advised that anything I do say may or may not be used in evidence, etc etc… "Yeah yeah", I mumbled, "and that nonce continues to be free because the CPS based their decision on a written mistake, allowing him walk free,"

So the Police help the perpetrator…again… and again, and again.

So, I was warned to make the house safe etc because I was going to be a while down the station. I was done and ready to go. .but couldn't because they were waiting for another vehicle, a van to 'transfer this prisoner' to Wiltshire Police Station. I said "What's the point of bunging me in a van, when I can quite safely sit in your car?" Procedure.

I was slowly beginning to nearly cack m'self, at the claustrophobic thought of being in that dog cage at the back of the van when I saw it arrive. I asked if I could "sit in the front instead, or just go in the car, in fact I'll take my car and meet you there promise?" Hell would've frozen over before getting that wish granted. I then said, "Ok…Please don't make me wear the handcuffs then?" It's still a claustrophobic feeling, being restricted from movement. I was allowed that much.

So clumsily, and funnily, I climbed and rolled into the back of their van, and had the door slammed on me. It seems to be quite a regular thing throughout the judicial system, these doors being slammed on people. So, off we went, noisily, I mean, how loud do those cage vans need to be!?

I absolutely dreaded the thought of anyone crashing into the back of this cage, because I was sat against the inner cage door, and one move to the right, I was sat against the main back doors. If anyone crashed into the back of us, I would've been coarsely grated.

So there was I, chauffeur driven, feeling like a German Shepherd dog en route to Wiltshire nick. I was going to start barking, but whenever I seriously thought I'd do it, I couldn't stop grinning, plus, I had to occupy myself trying to undo the cage lock for a bit of mindfulness out of claustrophobia.

I arrived at check in, feeling like a dwarf now, because the check in desk is like five foot six ish, level with my height. The desk guy, looks down to little ol' me, still in my wellies, and takes my details, and can't remember if it was there or later, I had the charge read out to me.

After about half an hour, I was searched, then shown to my room.

Well, taken to the cells, told to remove my wellies, where the cell door was…you guessed it… slammed on me.

I asked about having my ipod with me, but wasn't allowed in case I harmed myself with it. They must've heard about my singing.

I asked for a pen and paper. I was allowed to write, only with a pencil though. That's fine, I like writing so don't mind what I use.

I worked on mindfulness to avoid claustrophobic moments. The walls are a motley bumpy stuff like portafleck, which is like inside corridors and stairwells in tower blocks etc.

Up at the window to the left of what one might call a window casing. I saw three small dents closer together. I couldn't resist drawing round them, to produce an Aliens' face. I guess it's still there. It was mindfulness, at its most creative under the circumstances.

I did write on the paper provided to me as well though;

- "…So shitface not only gets away with sexually abusing me, he now believes he's the innocent one.
- I send/post by hand, letters of my anger, at the fact that he's sitting pretty, probably laughing at me, for us sleeping together when I was 6 or 5, he was 33, and escaping conviction… 12 charges, gross indecent assault to a child under 13? Or Indecent assaults. Never mind the attempting to rape me on the settee.
- This is a day, of me being the criminal, for my reaction to the impact the CPS cancelling the trial, based on mistakes, had on me.
- Waiting for ever for the evidence of my counselling, when I was much younger.
- I'm not on some bandwagon of others' historical sexual abuse cases. I only want justice for what he's done to me from the ages of 5 to 15 years.
- If I want to let him know just what a filthy, lying cunt he is, then I think I should be allowed to."

I did add basically the same angry stuff in bullet points under this writing. I also briefly summed up my day. For writing letters;

- Arrested done
- Locked in a cell done
- Finger prints done
- Photograph/mugshots done
- DNA Swabs done
- Questioned done

During my time in there, I was questioned by a couple of women at different times. I think one was for the Mental Health and I can't remember who the other one was from. I could only tell them, this is just the beginning. I'm going with the flow, and the best is yet to come.

I was offered a Duty Solicitor. I had a brief meeting with him in an interview room before being interviewed by two Police women. Oh boy! The more my Duty Solicitor and I spoke, the more I was being taught self-defence, physically doing moves to protect myself, in this interview room. It's about 50 years too late.

We started the interview. Where basically they read the letters out and mentioned about the phone calls at three a.m etc. I was asked, if I'd made those phone calls. I couldn't keep my face straight so admitted it.

I was asked why I made those calls at that time, and not speak to him when he answered. I told them, "When I'm awake at that time, it's because I had a nightmare about him. Well if I can't be allowed to sleep, because of him, I ain't letting him sleep"

This recorded interview went on, and at the end of it, I was bailed and had to report to them about a month later, to see if I was going to court or be cautioned, and told to stay away from my perpetrator. I was called during that month to be advised they're giving me a caution, which I had at another Wiltshire Police Station.

It's A Bit Like Stockholm Syndrome.

IMAGINE BEING A young kid again, when you've been up to mischief, but didn't realise it's wrong because you're innocent, and when very young, you didn't actually understand differences between right and wrong. Like waking up, figuring out what to do, and making games from items around the house, then someone roared at you for it, and frightened you that much, that you feared using your initiative, exploration and communication, but you still had to look up to that roaring face and respect it.

Amongst my 'familys' crumbling, I was still always answerable to dads' roaring and needs. He would reckon himself highly, lecture me and the two brothers, often telling us the wrong *we* done, even whilst he abused me and cleared off with Mums' best friend during Mums' breakdown after losing a baby during the birth.

He, who I had to shut my mouth for because of '*his*' wrong doing, of swiping my childhood from me, whilst perving on me, forcing me into no confidence, and sabotaging my social and educational growth etc etc..

So how, and why the hell did I still be the good Daughter?

I mentioned it's a bit like Stockholm Syndrome because it resembles the victim falling prey to and siding with, or needing to feel closer to the kidnapper (or the one in control), because it feels safer to keep in with them. They have total control over you and anyone else outside

103

this bubble is less able to protect you now, so you shut up and work with your main controller.

I hated my regular incidents of sex abuse, but my dad was the highest person in my life, my owner and controller. I had nobody to help me escape his selfish, revolting order, so I had to grin and bear it. I still had to look up to him as if everything was as decent and normal as any non-sex abuse father/Daughter relationship must have been.

Outside the flat, we probably appeared as normal as any other family in the father/Daughter sense. Inside the flat, dad was my owner and I was his sexual satisfaction. I was 'daddys' girl', then once done, he was orderly in telling me it's our secret. I was keeping 'in' with him and this secret. I'd witnessed his temper against Mum and I feared all that against me. There was nowhere to hide. It was safer to do what I was told, during and after our sex.

Without this sounding contradictory…When the neighbours came to get dad out of our flat that time and they were fighting and scuffling in our flat in the hallway. I felt like it was a bit sad seeing dad getting a hiding. I think that must have been because of the 'daddys' girl' hold he had on me then. I can't describe it as a bond because he never made me feel bonded with him, he didn't make me feel proud of him for anything or any kind of emotional ties. Straight after he was taken out of the flat, I felt like chains had been cut from me.

With that strike of luck for me, freedom from sex abuse, one would've thought it was over for good and I was safe. No, I went back to him by visiting him at Rose's flat, actually sneaking over there to them so that Mum wouldn't know. I guess that's because I wanted to hear 'daddys' girl'.

I wanted to hear words that made me feel wanted and missed by someone. There wasn't any of those sort of words from Mum when she returned, hence the sneaking to Rose's flat, but I never did get the verbal attention I was really after.

The dad/Daughter relationship or should I say sex connection was like a film set in which you left the scene, in my case stopped contact with dad for several months, then start talking again, (re-enter the scene), but with him, the autocue was stuck, he'd repeat his lectures at me. He'd waffle the same old shit, confirming we're not good or clean enough, why? because we were dragged up by Mum single handedly. Why? because *he* cleared off, which left me wearing clothes given to Mum, from the Womens' Royal Voluntary Service.

On rare occasions, he'd visit us at the house in Crayford Kent. I hated those times, with Rose turning up with him, rubbing salt in the wounds for Mum. They'd scan the living room looking down their noses at it. I'd either go upstairs a few seconds before they knock, or go out for a while. If I'd been caught in my tracks, dad would ask me 20 questions, and like an idiot, I'd end up talking to him as if he's someone special, I'd actually look up to him and even show him respect, even though he'd far from earned any. When I spoke with him, I'd smile, yet it was pure tension, and nervousness, then the headaches and nose bleeds would start again. Yet, after all that he'd done to me, all his sexual abuse, lies, power over me, the bullshittin' hypocrite, still made me feel I had to look up to him because he's 'dad'. It was like that all through his rule, and every time we fell out, he'd tell the bro's "Oh, she's in one of her 'not talking' moods again". Then after a few weeks, months, even years, we'd be back on talking terms again. I just don't know why I let it happen again. Even when we did talk again, he'd still stroke Rose's' arse in front of me, saying "look at that". Or pull faces, whilst staring at my breasts, and I still respected the twat.

He never has, and never will grow out of the slimy, perverted ways.

Here's an example: In the recent years, we moved to a house about 6 miles from him. India and I did regular shopping, cleaning and ironing for him for 'pocket money'.

On one particular store visit, dad with us, he walked towards an area where a woman was standing still, whilst browsing. He got up close to her, and moved his hand towards her backside, as if to cup his hand against it but only a couple of inches away from her. If she had turned around, he would've unavoidably touched her. In another part of the same store, a different woman thanked him for moving out of her way, he replied (words to this effect.) "That's alright as long as we can go out sometime". I said in a raised voice "dad!". He had nothing to say after that, because he'd seen I was really annoyed with him.

He used to tell us what the Doctor had said about one of his many ailments, He didn't just say about his health though, he'd describe the narrowness of her figure, the shortness of her skirt, how she walked, and the pathetic 'old man' chat up lines he'd say. The guy's a freak!.

So we'd talk for a few months or weeks, then fall out for a while, and it's never been because he's right, as much as he'd like to believe he was. It's been because of various reasons. Once was when I told him straight, during a phone call, where he agreed to not contact me, he must've been worried about me going to the Police. Another time was when he'd sit there watching India hoovering, then start saying about how much I'm like Mum, then start slating Mum, telling me she didn't like doing housework, or about Mum putting money under the top of the fridge, saying things like "Ah yeah, she had plenty of bloody money there." Yes, it was to get our food and pay the bills and it didn't come from him, because he wasn't paying her, but rather than be angry, I didn't have the guts to fall out with him there and then. I chickened out of it and made it light hearted, but then I had to listen to his crap about him not paying maintenance being someone else's fault in the courts' fines room. Of course it wasn't dads' fault, so why get it reduced to £1 per month for us three then huh? He actually told me that, then laughed. It's because he preferred paying for Rose's sons' food and clothing, her bingo nights and the mortgage etc. And I *still* looked up to him, confirming his ownership of my mind and body but only until our final fallout.

All those years of fear, intimidation, sex and ownership upon me by him, and I still listened to him, empathised and looked up to him. His ruling of my life was only until relatively recently though, when I finally blew my stack and pressed charges against him.

They Knew ...

I REQUESTED A copy of one of my letters to dad, from the Police Headquarters Disclosure Unit and was pleased to have obtained it successfully. I was grinning big time about the extras that came with it, which I didn't expect but found it good book fodder. It was copies of the statements by my brothers, step sister and the nonce himself, dad. I read through them with some disgust but no surprise at their bullshit during questioning. I was glad to have this unexpected chapter arrive in the post, and during typing it in, I edited my replies in amongst their lies. If I'd managed to get this case to trial, I'm sure these statements would've been read out and whichever liar was in the dock at the time would be further questioned on their statement. I would've hoped to have had my say on their lies then. But seeing as it didn't get to trial, and the sex crimes still stand, my replies here are what I also didn't get the chance to say in the set, then cancelled trial. Nonce dad's statement has more thorough questions and answers through it. Then my replies to them are in *italic*. The other statements haven't got the questions on them. I just wrote what's been said by the brothers and stepsister, then my answers on them.

STATEMENT ONE...

The eldest brother did a statement towards this case.

He couldn't talk about dad in the truthful sense, because he refused to accept what I've been blurting out across the years as being the truth. Rather than that, he said;

"Believes the allegations are false, and did not think there are any grounds for these allegations".

He clearly didn't listen to me across the years, nor understand those tantrums I had when I often said "What dad done to me" during any conversations about dad.

Maybe like many others in families where a parent has abused a sibling, the other untouched family members don't want to believe that a parent is a nonce.

Yet he went on to say;

"They (allegations) may have been from her counselling sessions" as I do recall her saying to me 'My counsellor says dad abused me'"...

I probably said that because it's something to do with me being sexually abused by dad.

He also states;

"Eliza made these allegations, and then my father decided to not have Eliza in his will"

Yes, that's correct. I'd had enough of dads' perving, and rebelled about it, before he took me out of his stupid will.

He went on;

"I am aware of an apology to her (me) as an adult. I have been told by my father that he had a brief conversation with Eliza during a car trip, when she said she forgave him for masturbating and that he said sorry to her"

Yet again, he even believes dad even after dad told him about apologising to me for masturbating, but even when dad falsely admits to him he was masturbating in my presence as a child, didn't my brother think on from that!? And no, dad didn't actually masturbate in front of me... That's dads' cover up of me forgiving him for the sex abuse. I masturbated dad!.

This eldest brother also once told me re- dad abusing me, "dad wouldn't do that, and I can't see that happening". That was during one of my non-speaking times to dad.

I also mentioned to him some other annoyance about dad in 2001 starting with "Stepsisters' old man" (meaning dad), then the eldest brother butted in saying "Don't you mean Dad?" I told him, "Well he ain't my dad anymore after what he done to me. He never brought us up either". The brother became his bolshy self again, telling me "Yeah well he's still dad whatever's happened, so if you can't say anything good about him, then I'm not going to be in contact with you!" 'Whatever's happened' ay?

Another of his strops concerning dad, was when I'd told my other brother about me not wanting to know dad.

Elder brother questioned me, saying,

"What's this I hear you said something about dad, you not wanting to know if he passed away?" So I told him straight, I said "No, if the old man pops his clogs, I don't want to know about it, and don't want anything to do with him".

He said "Look, everything he done wrong was years ago, and don't be so bloody nasty, and on that note, I've nothing to say to you anymore!" Wow, that's a worry for me from the golden boy!. There's *so* nothing wrong with dad then, that this same elder brother wouldn't let his daughter call Rose 'Nan'. Because she wasn't our mum, and she was who dad cleared off with, and it annoyed our nasty dad.

He went on, in his statement to say;

"I am very concerned for my fathers' health because of *this*. He's elderly and lives on his own, this is all very stressful".

Oh my! How benevolent of him.

Elderly? Lives on his own? Stressful, huh? Just so you know… He was about thirty-three years old, a mature adult when he chose to start abusing me. He knew right from wrong don't you think? I live with this sex abuse crap in my head daily, and so probably does dad from his criminal, dirty moves on me, and him living on his own is nothing, he has you supporters comforting and mollycoddling him on the phone weekly. And as for stressful, I've had Complex PTSD since the age of six. Why? Because of what that disgusting old bastard you're defending, done to me.

STATEMENT TWO…

Now it's onto the other brother's' statement. He knows a certain amount of the abuse that happened. But he too done a supportive statement about dad, and says;

"I never had a reason to challenge my father about his behaviour with Eliza at bath time."

Er knock knock! "What's going on in there and why's the light off!?" I know he remembers it.

He didn't speak to dad for many years after his and mums' separation when dad cleared off with Rose. I mostly used to feel supported and encouraged by him, especially when he or I had fallen out with the eldest brother, and/or dad. However, I'm the one who's been completely shat on by him now, thanks to his supportive statement.

It was around about the time I'd fell out with eldest brother in 2001. I said to the youngest brother;

"Yeah, all sorts was going on between me and dad at the flat in the 60's and their house 70's. Do you remember I was in the bathroom with dad, and the light was off, and door locked, then you banged on the bathroom door, asking what's going on in there and why's the light off?"

He told me, "Yeah, vaguely I do". I said, "I remember it clearly. That's when it was all happening, and in dads' bedroom".

Well, he chose to not remember it when doing his statement.

When I first reminded him about it, I was in a public phone box in a Wiltshire town centre, trying to explain some of the delicate descriptions, yet trying to explain it quietly to avoid anyone overhearing me. I'd told him more of what went on, where, and how often things were happening, and said,

"I'm having counselling for it all because my head's in a mess".

His reply to that was;

"Yeah, but dad isn't getting any younger is he, and it was years ago that it happened, and to be honest I think you're over reacting".

I never forgot that reply. Thanks for that, "He's not getting any younger?"

He was an adult when I was in the infants' school when he was first abusing me.

Thanks for your concerns for dad the nonce, instead of your sibling/victim. One fine brother you turned out to be aswell.

He then went on to slate me by saying,

"She used the family for food and money, as she did with everyone".

Fact is, I wasn't getting money from India's' father until she was thirteen. So, whenever I done a huge cook out for when one of the brothers and their families turned up, they'd bring a bit of food over to contribute voluntarily, unless I asked for anything specific if I needed it for the cook out and if I borrowed any money, I paid it back. I was the only lone parent out of us three but I still always paid my way. Where he got the thought of me using 'everyone' for food and money is confusing. I wasn't even in touch with anyone else apart from my employers and work colleagues. Anyway, what do his lies matter? They're just his tactics to avoid the truth being said to the CID.

He then went on further about the money, this time stating,

"She had money off dad for the business, car and furniture for the house".

Right, for a start, I have had the same furniture for years, which has been upcycled a few times, beautifully, even if I do say so myself. Any money off dad was loaned to me and it all got paid back, unless it was cleaning and ironing pocket money. He didn't loan me anything towards the business, I had a business loan via the Jobcentre.

This brother also stated;

"My dad and Eliza fell out over a comment he made to India. Eliza sent a letter to dad, the contents I do not know but it really upset him. She *then* got more money for a Range Rover".

I didn't get money for any Range Rover, I borrowed a small amount towards a second hand Land Rover, which he got back a couple of months after. Then I needed to get that letter to dad. We then had the row on the phone about the contents of my letter, and I haven't had anything to do with him since, because he's a nonce.

Then this brother said,

"I think that she feeds him (dad) with suggestions, as he has memory problems after an accident".

That one lost me, god knows what I'm meant to have suggested. That accident was approximately 1977. The only problem dad's got is a selective memory. He remembers me being a good baby sleeping right through at night, yet the sex abuse seems to escape his memory.

He finished his statement saying;

"I do not recall any behaviour I would describe as untoward".

How sad that a sibling, who I always considered a brave and strong child himself during his own rough upbringing, and who faced up to dad during one of dads' disgusting, criminal incidents upon me, who now can't even admit it. How sad indeed.

This statement is nothing but a weak and cheap, masking over of the truth, by slating me about my finances during the earlier days of lone parenting, yet during those times, most nicer people told me my Daughter India is a real credit to me, but this brother decides to twist my lone parenting struggles against me, in order to duck out of admitting he witnessed the sex abuse in the bathroom.

Why else did he go on about something irrelevant to this case? I'm not the money grabbing person he has portrayed me as, I've always worked, even since India was 6 months of age. I've got very small debts, which are still being paid, and I never use credit cards. I've only ever borrowed twenty pounds off this brothers' wife, when India needed something I'd forgotten to purchase, towards her new secondary school uniform, and I sent a postal order for twenty pounds back in the post the following week.

So, yes this statement is one empty, irrelevant attempt to divert from the lawful truth.

This brother does know what went on, but he's lied to protect dad the sex abuser.

STATEMENT DAD...

Pages of questions, and lies throughout the majority of his answers, but what else could I expect from this guilty lowlife. I'll enter some of the questions from Laura/CID, and dad's' answers to them, then my replies after some of his answers.

This is the only way I can respond to dad's' statement as if the trial had gone ahead.

The only questions I'm not copying into this, are about addresses, confirmation of name and the general life story ie divorces and dad's adultery.

C 1,2,3 etc   = CID questions

D   = Dad

Italics   = My response

C1 "When you were still with your first wife then, tell me about your relationship with Eliza then".

D"Well it was no different to any other father in an average good family. She was a sulky little devil at times, you know, she could sulk, which was inherited from her late mum Lord rest her, but other than that, I think I know what led up to this, and I'm going to state it now with this on".

C2 "Yes absolutely".

He then goes on about when we met up after I'd just had India, 1994, and the arrangement to pick us up from Kent and take us to their place in Wiltshire for a few days. But he waffled on about the route he took. He went on...

D "I pulled in to have a smoke and all of a sudden she (Eliza) said "I forgive you dad". "I thought, did I hear right so I said what's that love, she said "I forgive you". I said, what, for breaking up with your mum? And she said "No" I said well what? She said "For masturbating". I said what the hell are you on about? She said "That night in bed". She said "You let me sleep with you, and I asked you where babies come from". I said yes, and if your memory's clear you'll remember which may have been a bit of a silly thing to do, but it was just one of those things, I come (climbed?) over the top of her, didn't touch any part of her and I said to her, 'What's between daddys' legs, goes between mummy's' legs anything else ask your mother'. and I got back on my side to go to sleep. She said later then I masturbated, which I denied. She insisted on it so I thought to myself is there any possibility I could do it and can't remember? Because I have lost certain things in the past and got a very severe fractured skull"

He is avoiding the subject that's approaching and saying anything to divert from the truth. It was no different to any other father in the average family where sex abuse took place. One doesn't inherit sulking, but there's a common factor why mum and I may have sulked. Look in the mirror you idiot! I didn't say I'd forgiven him for masturbating. He's lying straight away. I was saying I forgive him for what happened in the flat (sexually abusing me). I had Complex PTSD even then because of his selfish behaviour on me and attempting to rape me. And in mum's' defence, and just to remind dad, he cleared off with Rose, who was mums' best friend, at the same time as mum suffered the still birth of my sister, you heartless bastard.

What I actually said "I forgive you for what you done to me but can't for what you done to mum". His reply was "What was that?". I said "Me in the flat with you I forgive, but mum didn't have anyone to help her when she lost the baby did she", fact. He said "Ah right, yeah ye mother was a lovely woman". That was what was said during that driving break.

When we got to his place, he said he couldn't remember anything back in the flat about me, due to that bang on the head, and cried and said "Sorry if I hurt you". He remembered then, and remembers now full well what he done to me in that flat and other house.

115

That was one of the phases of us talking again and I felt up to saying I forgive him, thinking and hoping the abuse memories would slip away whilst we could start to get on fine.

He also added in that same statement answer, about the fall out over him telling India not to tell me. He added

D "Eliza, my Daughter, could be very, very prudish as her mum, unfortunately, and I then said, Oh you'd better not tell your mum I asked were you behaving yourself cos she may take it the wrong way. I didn't get any call but when I got up in the morning, there was a letter through my door and I wish to god I kept it. I tore it up in disgust to be quite honest"

That letter he's referring to is in this book, and we know what he meant by asking "behaving herself?" Remember what I wrote about that time in his kitchen, when he wouldn't leave the subject of India and her partners' private life? He tried every angle to get me to talk about whether they're having sex, to which I replied It's not ours or anyone else's business and I don't want to talk about it. He was desperate to get me to talk about it. I am far from interested in their private lives, and as for saying about my mum being prudish well, I preferred that over a noncing parent!

C3 "So as far as you're aware, these are two separate incidents many years apart when"…

D "She phoned up, Oh I can't remember, it's going back some time after this incident and I can't remember what it's to do with but I just asked her if she was alright. I'm acting with no nastiness towards her although I was sick at what she said, and I said I can't believe you wrote me such a letter, I said how could you do that? and she says what about the bathroom, I said what lies are you making up now? And I put the phone down and that's the last I've heard of her since But then after that I was so shocked, I racked my brains, I thought god, have I forgotten something or not? I thought to myself no I'm not gonna blame this…There's things I can't remember, she said on the phone about the bathroom. I thought, I've got to remember what was going on, and then it clicked, It took me four hours of constant thought then I phoned up my eldest son and told him, your mothers' attitude and rule was mum's wash the girls and dad's wash the boys, and the only time that it was Eliza, was when their mother wasn't there for a bath night, when we were estranged and she moved round her sisters for three or four months and then I used to get the soap, the towel, the flannel and her pyjamas, pour her bath, and say don't be too long because your brothers got to have their bath yet, and that was it. That's the only two incidents that I can recall that she's obviously saying other things I don't know but as I say I won't go further with that because I can't, that's all that happened. I'm being perfectly honest about it"..

He doesn't know 'Perfectly honest' about anything. He was in the bathroom with me every time mum was away, which I've learned is about four months, and I was wanking him off every time, as soon as that bloody door was locked.

C4 "So I want you to concentrate on those four months or so while you were looking after the children".

D "Yes".

C5... "And about routines, you've already touched on it a little bit so up until your wife left, you sorted out the boys, your wife sorted out Eliza".

D "Yes".

C6 "So when your first wife was out of the way, tell me what would happen about bath times with Eliza?"

D "Exactly what I've just said, I'd get the towel, the flannel her pyjamas, the soap, run the bath for her and i'd say right, in you go sweetheart, don't take too long because your brothers got to have their bath, and then I'd close the door, and sometimes she'd say leave it open a bit dad, so I'd leave it open".

Lies. He must have me in a muddle with my Stepsister because he never got the jamas and soap etc. I had the poodle dog, shaped bubble bath when he stayed in the bathroom with me.

C7 "So when you closed the door, were you inside the bathroom or outside the bathroom?"

D "I would go outside, outside yeah".

Lying bastard.

C8 "And when you saw her next, how would she be dressed?"

D "When she come out, she'd dried herself, in her pyjamas she'd come out in her pyjamas".

C9 "And roughly how old was Eliza at that age?"

D "Between nine and ten I'd say, because it was not long after that when the mother came back and she wanted me out, So I didn't hesitate".

Going on what classes I was in, Miss H, to Mrs B' classes, makes me about five to six years of age. And then two other classes including a Mrs W, from that takes me up to seven years of age, then I moved into Colyers' Lane School about aged eight when it opened.

C10 "So did anything more than what you've described ever happen in the bathroom with you?"

D "Nothing, whatsoever."

Liar.

C1 "And your Daughter?"

D "Nothing whatsoever, that's why I'm so shocked with what she's come out with. She's come out with that latest one. She'd never ever mentioned anything like that, even when she said that night in the car about I forgive you. Why didn't she bring it up then as well?"

I wasn't up to confronting him with the many detailed explanations of his sex abuse then, because so much had gone on, and I was gutless to confront him fully about it, especially as we'd just got talking again. It was just as well it wasn't all brought out then because I had two resurfaced memories of his sex abuse incidents since that day. 'Nothing whatsoever' ay? Bloody liar.

C12 "That same period of time then, those sort of four months while you were trying to do the work and looking after the children?"

D "Yeah?"

C13 "What were the sleeping arrangements like in the flat?"

He went on and on about the layout of the flat and pointed out where my bedroom was.

C14..."Bedtime routines then, about that time, so you were looking after the three children by yourself, Whereabouts did Eliza sleep?"

D "Well in her bedroom".

C15... "In her own bedroom?"

D "In her own bedroom yeah. There was only one night ever she wanted to come in and sleep in my bed and I allowed her one night and that's all I said, one night."

I definitely remember the bedtime hand relief, and can picture him on top of me now but this might be the flashes of the settee attempted/successful rape. Or did he rape me in their bed?? I hope there isn't any more resurfaced memories due, because he's gunna need some serious surgery if I do remember something else.

C16 "So one night, and was the occasion where you described?"

D "When she asked that question, well I've already said it on there anyway."

C17 "And that was on that occasion?"

D "That one occasion and one occasion only. No touching whatsoever, no molesting whatsoever. It might have been very foolish of me as a very young dad but that's the best way I could explain it, I didn't want to go into any further details, and that's why I said she'd have to ask her mother."

Lying, evil bastard.

He goes on to other stuff about who we've spoken with years ago, because there's two people who spoke with me, who used to visit dad once a month, Jehovah's' Witnesses people. They once asked me in their own gentle way, if dad touches me up,. I'd said "No" because it's our secret. I don't know if mum had thought that something sinister was going on like it was, then asked them to ask me, or maybe I'd said something innocently, which mum picked up on during these days in the flats. So why did she leave me with him if that's the case?

So the interview with wanker continues…

C18 "What I think I'll do now is just outline what her allegations are that she's brought to the Police."

D "Yes please."

C19 "There's a fair bit, I've typed it all up so I've tried to be brief, summarise it a little bit. Now she talks about and incident in the bathroom, she thinks she might be little, about five or six years of age. That's her memory, but I think it was before your wife, it was about the time your wife left, she talks about she doesn't know where her mum went, her mum just disappeared, she didn't really understand so".

D "No, she was nine years old when the mum went round to her sister".

C20 "So even at nine years old, she's saying mum disappeared no one explained it very well to her and she was aware that her mum was round her aunties and that like you've explained (Rose) across the road helped out when you were working so that bit we agree on. What she does say is she talks about incidents in the bathroom. Now she talks about it being over a period of about two years, that's her recollection. If I go exactly into her account, she says that while she was in the bath you would remain in the bathroom with her. Do you remember that?"

D "Never, that's one thing I never done".

Will this nonce ever stop lying!?

C21 "I'm just gunna try and find it on her interview so I can use her words. Right, she says here, She'd have been between the ages of five and nine but she says about the ages of five years old she had been naked in the bath. Dad used to tell her to put her shoulders forward, and make what she called a 'fat cleavage', as she was chubby, so she was asked to sort of squeeze her arms together so she's saying it was. So she remembers that incident."

D "That is totally untrue".

Liar.

C22 "Have you ever asked her to do anything like that?"

d… "Never, ever, whatsoever. I assume that the earlier age that she's stating here, I cannot see the mother allowing me in the bathroom. There was no way she would allow me in there because she was a strong believer in mum's washed girls, dad's washed boys and you didn't argue with her".

Mum was in hospital for something else for a while aswell, maybe it's during that time he was doing the bathroom sex abuse. I think mum had veins stripped from her legs.

C23 "She says about the very first time, she tries to recall the very first time anything like this happened and I'll read it from her interview. It says, 'It was like I was laughing at it cos I'd never really seen one before, I just started giggling and found it funny. I didn't think anything was wrong because it was dad. I was in the bath. I was using my bubble bath. I think dad said something like "Do you want to play with this?", and she's talking about you taking your penis out of your trousers while she's in the bath. Did you ever do that with Eliza?"

D "Never, never ever".

Liar.

C24 "She said, "He said play with it like this. She says you got your penis out and what she now knows that you had an erection. She didn't obviously know at that age".

D "I know why she's done it. But I'm not gunna say it at this time. I've just fell in"…

C25 "It's your chance to explain anything, if you think it's important please tell us".

D "I cut her out of my will and she phoned up. The brother phoned her just for the weekly chat, and she said she'd contest it with all her might".

If I'd brought all my rough childhood out in a video statement because of being cut out of his poxy will, all this fall out and court business would've happened several years before when we'd had another one of our big fall outs when he cut me out of the will after that row. I've brought it all out onto a video statement because I'm telling the truth and nothing but. He's taking wide circles around the truth, and latching onto any excuse to dis me and my mum, in order to avoid his filthy behaviour being brought to justice.

C26 "So you think that the reason behind her coming forward?"

D "I'd say that the majority of it because I've helped her out so much with money since she moved down here and that's what she's lost by getting upset over what I've said to her daughter; (Are you behaving yourself). She took it completely wrong and made me, tried to make me, call me in the letter a sexual perve that was the actual words she used, and that's what's blown this up".

No it bloody wasn't the reason behind me coming forward, not even close. I was cut out of the will because of the letter and fall out. The letter was triggered by him acting pervy, trying to get me and India to talk about sex to him. I was at my wits end with flashes of sex with dad, and now dad wants to talk of sex, and him being the creepy lowlife when we were doing his cleaning and ironing. I'd had enough, and him saying that to India on the phone, was the end for me.

C27 "Well she describes some incidents in the bathroom where she's saying she's naked in the bath and that you're stood at the side of the bath, and she says that you take hold of her wrist and you put it (hand), on your penis and you assist her in masturbating you basically. She says that you then ejaculated while she was in the bath, and that she had to wash her hands while she was in the bath, and she says it was horrible and it became a regular habit".

D "She's got a brilliant but dirty imagination".

Another blurt to escape the truth.

C28 "Is there any time that, you know, maybe"..

D "Never once have I ever exposed myself to her or any of my children".

I wish the truth drug testing in the Midlands, would happen down here.

C29 "I was about to ask, you know, was there any time that you perhaps you went to the toilet while she was in the bath but it was a separate bath and toilet".

D "No".

C30 "and that was about the same time she was asked to make her fat cleavage, cos she said she was chubby, and she's saying that the first time it happened she was told just to hold it and then had to, was asked to keep rubbing it up and down, talking about your penis. She stated that at the time she thought it was different and that she thought it was funny but she was asked to keep it: you told her to keep it daddys' little secret. Did you ever tell her to keep a secret?"

D "Never, ever, never. Nothing like that ever happened whatsoever".

Nonce can't think of anything else to say, fearing he'll drop himself in it.

C31 "She talked about, you know, using a flannel and I think you said that you laid flannels out and pyjamas out and towels out for her. So that's one, and it's not one incident let's be clear of that, she's saying it became fairly regular over a period of time that she was asked to masturbate you while she was laying in the bath. Did that ever happen?"

D "Never, never once. Because the door was usually left open, even when the lads went for their bath cos the two of them up to a certain age, the two of them used to get in together and have their bath, it saved time and everything for getting them ready for bed but, and especially if that was the period when their mother was there and the two lads were there".

Well mum wasn't there, and he's diverting away from the point of the question again.

C32 "Well you're saying it was only over a period of four months".

D "The only time that bathroom door was ever closed was if my wife was having a bath or I was having a bath, that's the only time it was ever closed and locked. It sickens me this, what she's said, it really sickens me".

All he's doing is going all round the houses from the brunt of any questions, by talking about how he feels as usual, and bringing it all back to when mum was there.

C33 "Right that's one particular type of incident she's describing alright".

D "Yes I know".

C34 "She's talking about other incidents that she says that she slept in the bed with you fairly regularly after your wife left".

D "One night only, I only allowed one night".

C35 "Now her recollection is that it was quite regular".

D "Never"

'Never', is that his favourite escape the truth word?

C36 "And she says, she says that she remembers sleeping next to you in, in the double bed in your bedroom and she says she thinks, she doesn't know how it started but she thinks that she may be sort of cuddled over into you, maybe putting her hand on you or something and you then turned round and got her to hold your penis and masturbate you while you were in bed".

D "What a vile woman".

Yes, the truth hurts doesn't it… Turning it all round to me is all you can think of isn't it.

C37 "She then says that you ejaculated whilst you were in the bed and that she would have to wipe her hands on the hanky that was at the side of the bed and she has quite"… …

D "There is not truth whatsoever in that. I cannot believe that she's said things like that, or made them up, because that's what is every bit of this is; wild imagination".

You wished it was, We both know you're as guilty as hell don't we dad.

C38 "So she's saying it was more than one occasion, it was over a period of time and she shared the bed with you".

D "No, that one night only and if I wanted to hide it, I wouldn't just say the one night because I volunteered that before hearing this".

This guilty one is trying to earn innocence points. It was more than one occasion.

C39 "Yeah, and she does, I'm trying to find it in her account cos I've got quite a lot, she does talk about that one account about daddy sticks this inside mummy, I'm just trying to find where she talks about it, so if you bear with me just for a minute".

D "Yeah yeah".

C40 "So in relation to sleeping with you, she said, Eliza didn't know whether she could ask, ask if she could sleep in the bed. She couldn't remember her dad telling her to but I just, she just usually felt lost because she was missing her mum. She had her own single bed in the little box room in the flat but she was certain that this, all this happened when her mum disappeared, or was not around. She said, Eliza was sleeping with her dad in the double bed, she would normally wear flannelette pyjamas and she thought her dad would wear pants. She could recall the first time it happened in the bed. "I was just laying there he had his back to me. I sort of turned into him I think, I was just feeling not sure, I think I touched his hip, and he said do you want this?. Never sort of say no to him." I'm reading some typing here, she felt like she couldn't say no to you it felt like it was a request yet it felt like an order as well".

D "To be quite honest, I don't want to listen to any more of this. I'm disgusted by it absolutely disgusted. I never thought she'd go to them extremes to be vindictive, that's the word, vindictive".

Yep, the truth is hitting him like a cricket bat! He's "absolutely disgusted", yes it's all about how he feels again, and "doesn't want to listen to any more of this". He can't listen to the truth of his own disgusting behaviour. Weak, lame and cheap.

C41 "I'm just reading her account, I'm just trying to find the bit where she describes you about 'sticking' 'mummy's and daddy's'. Right, she talks about, she says this is where it goes into mummy, do you remember that happening? So she said she has a conversation with you, exactly how you've described it that there was a conversation on the telephone in recent years and you said to her *"All I done was got on top of you and showed you what it was, and I said that goes into mummy there"*. I think he put it against me, I feel like he did but I can't be sure. But I feel like it happened. So this conversation about this is where it goes into mummy, do you remember the conversation happening? "Yes it was a kind of flashback", she says that the incident happened on the settee. "I do remember saying what's that" I do feel like there's some sort of thing against me. She's saying that Eliza is terrified and said that her dad's zip was undone she could see his erect penis, he was wearing dark trousers, his trousers were still on, she didn't know whether he had a top on or not. I remember it happening at our flat, my dad said *"You're a bleeding liar"* something like that *"I got on top of you and showed you, telling you that this goes into mummy or something like that"*. So you're describing a different account you're saying in the bedroom and she's describing it on the sofa.

D "Yes, yes, that was the bedroom. Never touched her anywhere, anywhere else. Never".

Oh that 'never' word again.. and looking back to what the last paragraph, what 'C' says, on lines three to six, he hasn't denied that he had exposed himself prior to saying "That goes into mummy there", and that was prior to the attempted or successful rape, on the settee… If there's a rape in the bed, it hasn't resurfaced yet, but I can get flashes of him on top of me in the bed too.

C42 "In relation to that one particular incident is there anything else you want to say about it?"

D "No just as I said the only two things that I've thought of when she said about the bathroom which is only last June it was, she hasn't been near since a year last May, when she said "what about the bathroom?", and I just thought, what the hell's she on about. I said "what lies are you thinking up now?" and felt so disgusted I just put the phone down because of having had that letter calling me a sexual perv' just a few weeks before".

He knew full well what I was on about in reference to 'the bathroom'.

C43 "Go right back to when she was little and you were in the bed and you said, you said about climbing over the top of her".

D "Which, I've already got on tape one".

C44 "What were you wearing at the time? What would you have worn to bed?"

D "If I remember, a pyjama jacket and a short pyjama thing that I used to wear, the type I used to wear when I used to have to work away sometimes".

C45 "So"…

D "But I had to change my job, that's why I went on the railway because of difficulties with the first wife".

C46 "So when you had the pyjama shorts on, did you have anything on underneath the shorts?"

D "No not usually. Same as if I wear pyjamas now, I just put my jama top on and my shorts on, that's if I wear them going to bed".

He wore pants.

C47…"So this one occasion you've got Eliza sleeping next to you, can you remember what she's wearing".

D "Just pyjamas, normal pyjamas".

C48… "So how did this conversation come about, that you then straddled her or went on top of her?"

D "Well as I said on tape one, that she just said how are babies made, so I climbed over the top, not touching any part of her, and I says, well what's between dad's legs, goes between mum's legs, anything else ask your mum, and I went back on my side and then went to sleep, but she accused me later of masturbating".

He's had time to program the words to repeat, I never once accused him of masturbating as I've explained, I did it for him, and he didn't deny exposing himself in C41.

C49 "Just go back to when you were in bed, so you've straddled over her, you've not touched her and when you said what goes on, what's between daddy's legs goes between mummy's legs".

D "Yeah".

C50 "Where was your penis at the time?"

D "Where it always is. Attached to me".

C51 "Yeah, no sorry, could she see your penis at that time?"

D "No way, no, there's no way she could see it.

Really? Well, on question C41, it clearly states the phone conversation…

"*So she said she has a conversation with you, exactly how you've described it, that there was a conversation on the telephone in recent years and you said to her "All I done was got on top of you and **showed you what it (penis) was**, and I said that goes into mummy there".*

He knows I've seen it and remembers all that I've had to do to him.

C52 "So it was still within your pyjamas?"

D "That was still within the pyjamas and when I say they're shorts, they're down to about the knee cos they're that type of pyjama thing that I had. I've still got some at home actually. Well different ones obviously now but I've got two or three sets indoors".

He wore pants

C53 "and at that time, how did you feel, sexually?"

D "Nothing, nothing I was just surprised that she asked I thought oh Christ, I don't wanna answer this, so that's the only thing I could think of, saying that to her and then turned right anything else ask your mum".

Liar..

C54 "So did you have an erection at the time?"

D "No, good god no, no".

Yes, good god, bloody YES! The only time you didn't have an erection was when I'd finished doing what you made me do. Acorn cock!

C55 "So that was all a one off occasion?"

D "A one off occasion, it may have been silly what I done but as I said to her in the car that night when she said about I'll forgive you and I said forgive me what do you mean forgive oh for mum and me breaking up and she said no, she said for masturbating and I said what do you mean masturbating, she said that night in bed. I said what the one night you were with me?"

Programed words again, let's face it, he's had long enough to make this rubbish up.

C56 "Are you aware, so do you remember doing that? So you obviously remember going over the top of her".

D "Yes".

C57 "And not touching her?".

D "Yes".

Liar!

C58 "But do you remember masturbating after that?"

D "No, but the only reason I said to her when she insisted, she said you're using this to block out memory of it and I said Eliza, I said 'if it's a case of I can remember that incident and not something two or three minutes later', I said 'and I've lost that bit, then if I did do it I am truly, truly sorry' and she said I'll forgive you dad, and I thought that's twice, I'm mean twice she's just said it".

He's going all round the houses again. He didn't masturbate, I done it for him, and on the settee, he tried or successfully raped me. I know he's remembering it because he's glued himself to words to avoid slipping up about it all.

C59 "Let me just move on then, she talks about interestingly enough, you talked about blowing raspberries on them as a baby, you liked to hear them laugh, I think that's what you said didn't you earlier on",

D "What, did I say that I did?"

C60 "You said you liked to blow raspberries on their tummies or their backsides when they were little and you liked to hear them laugh".

D "When they were tiny boys or girls, it didn't matter which".

C61 "Now at one point in her account, Eliza refers to something very similar. She remembers feeling quite envious of the boys, that you used to play sort of rough and tumble with the boys".

D "With them yeah I played a lot with them when I could".

C62 "And she felt a little bit left out cos that wasn't something that you did so much with her, and she's saying that on one occasion, she remembers rough and tumble with you in the lounge and you end up on the/she ends up on the settee and you're blowing raspberries on her tummy. She's not a baby, she's a little bit older than that".

D "Yeah".

He knows what's being asked next for sure.

C63 "but she says that you then have oral sex with her, that you lick her vagina. Did you at any time do anything like that?"

D "Look, that woman is sick, there's no doubt about it. I've never known anybody to stoop so low, to be so vindictive, and I don't want to answer any more questions, I'm just sickened by what she's saying".

Tough! You might not want to answer questions about what you done to me, but I had to live with what you done to me. How can you possibly be sickened? You're a cold and callous liar! As soon as the CID hit on the gory truth, it's 'Oh I don't want to do this anymore" Man up and admit what you done to me! I feel a need to say you're the sick one, but you're not sick, you're perverted.

C64 "** I have to, I do have to tell you what she says. If you choose not to answer them, that's fine".

D "I know, I know".

How the truth hurts ay.

C65 "Alright it's only right that you understand what she's come to the Police with".

D "I should have left her in the will, nothing like this would've happened".

Fucks' sake, that poxy will makes him think he rules the planet. I done the letter and we'd fallen out before he took my name off the will! He removed my name because of our fall out. This was always going to happen because he was still eyeing up females, and trying to get India and I to talk about sex basically, which was the decider. I'm 57 now. And him and our sex is still finding its way through my head.

C66 "She then talks about she's a little bit older, cos she talks about Rose, so that's the lady over the road".

D "Yeah".

C67 "Who, you eventually married. She then says that she remembers one occasion that she's over there, I think like you've described that she helped you out when you were trying to sort of bring them up on your own".

D "Yeah".

C68 "And she says that on one occasion when she's over the road at Rose's you say that, you know, Eliza's a little bit tired, she needs to get her head down and you take her and put her on Rose's bed and let her go with the intention of going to sleep. And she says on on that one occasion over in Rose's flat she had to masturbate you as she did regularly in the bed at home".

D "I tell you, my late wife would turn in her grave if she could hear this".

Oh boy, she must be spinning then, along with mum, your sister and your parents, now that they all probably know the truth in the spirit world.

C69 "So she says it's one incident that she remembers happening in Rose's".

D "There's absolutely no truth in it. The only time she was ever in that flat and Rose was alive at the time and she used to come up for her pocket money that I used to give her every week, some weeks it was two shillings and some weeks it was three shillings I mean that's what they got then, but she used to sneak up, she used to not let her mum see her cos her mum used to visit a neighbour further up and she was warned not to go near Rose and (shitface), Well, Rose and dad".

What I've said is the truth and nothing but. Everything I said on the video and wrote here, happened. Would I go to these lengths of a video statement, appearing in court and writing a book, so that I can state my truthful side of events if I was the liar? Everyone else has had their say, but this is my final voice in answer to those statements of lies.

C70 "She's talking about one particular incident where she remembers you, getting her to masturbate you".

D "No truth in it whatsoever"

Whatsoever ay? This is becoming a catalogue of lies from him.

C71 "She also says that she felt especially (word missing) around Rose's. whenever she visited Rose's flat you quite openly were inappropriate and would touch her breast over her clothing in front of Rose".

D "I remember an incident like that, I think she was about nineteen, twenty or eighteen, nineteen or something like that, she came with two female friends to borrow something from Rose. We were in ** Road then, it wasn't in the flat, and I'm a humorous person, I always have been and I know even in them days it was wrong, it would be wrong today but when she came in she seemed to be all up here like that, I'd not seen her like that before so"…

C72 "All uplifted?"

D "Yeah and I just went (noise made) like the old fashioned car horn. And she said dad don't do that I don't like it, I said sorry sweetheart, that's it. That was in the house. She came to borrow something off Rose I can't remember what it was".

I was wearing ordinary, horrible bra's, nothing like push up bra's, just ordinary, basic support. He isn't a humorous person at all, he's just a perve. Saying "It would be wrong today?" It was wrong since I was about two years of age, until about fifteen going on eighteen. And it was Rose screeching at dad about it, that embarrassed him enough to stop groping me, and he did not say sorry.

C73 "So Rose was there?"

D "Yes".

C74 "As were these two friends?"

D "Yeah".

C75 "When you did that honk honk was that actually over her breasts? Was it actually, did you touch it?"

D "No, I actually touched her, I went like (noise made) and that was it and she said don't dad, I said sorry love".

I didn't say anything but my face probably said enough.

C76 "So was that over her clothing or under her clothing?"

D "Over, over, her two friends were standing beside her. They laughed when I done it but to them it was comical but to her obviously it was a bit embarrassing I suppose so that's it, nothing like that happened again".

Nothing that you didn't get caught for at the time of each incident, apart from the bathroom door knocked on.

C77 "So what you need to understand is that's what Eliza's come to us with, she's described five particular, I won't say five separate incidents cos some of them were over a period of time".

D "Yeah".

C78 "Matters already discussed"..

C79. "Stated that he was unaware as to whether Eliza had received any counselling over the years but that he would not be surprised if she had, as her mother had been admitted to a Kent hospital for the mentally disturbed for two or three weeks at some time after they had separated and he thought that perhaps Eliza suffered with the same problems"..

Seriously!? Mum just thought w'hoo I'll go mental and get sectioned! And dad's made himself believe he's not at fault with that too. Just like he believes he's innocent in all this. He's actually the cause of so much bad gone on, from his actions upon me.

C80 "You went to the bedroom with her and you got Eliza to masturbate you and Rose was in the other room".

D "Boy, now that would be sailing close to the wind wouldn't it. That's disgusting it is".

You should know, you was there being wanked off by me!

C81 "Stated that *the reason he had cut Eliza from the will was because he had received the abusive letter calling him a sexual perve. It was after receiving this that he had removed her from his will.* He stated that he thought that Eliza had been informed by her older brother that she had been removed from the will. He stated that he had since reinstated Eliza into his will and that her older brother had also informed her of this. Clarified that he had cut her out of the will a week or two weeks after receiving the letter from her, he had told his daughter in Wiltshire of this and his two sons in Kent. Stated that Eliza had not said anything to him about this, they had never discussed it together. She had discussed it with her brothers and this had resulted in a slanging match between them. Since this there had been very little contact by Eliza. He stated that it had been around a year since contact between Eliza and her brothers".

So he tripped himself up, by now stating he cut me from the will after receiving the letter from me, which is the truth about me getting that letter to him, because he's constantly perving, and it was nothing to do with his bloody will.

C82 Confirmed that he would be willing to provide Police with a copy of his will, this included dates of the removal and the re addition of Eliza/Eliza to it.

C83 "Just looking through Eliza's account now it was, she says it was her youngest brother who came into the bathroom and saw you in the bathroom with her so I don't know if that makes any sense"... ...

D "What and saw me doing something with her?"

C84 "Well, just in the bathroom with her and challenged why you were in the bathroom with her".

D Confirmed that Elizas' brothers numbers were in a telephone book in his home.

Nothing further to add, change or clarify.

So, it's clear that my dad is totally gutless, and a liar

He says he knows why I've brought all this up to the Police, is because he'd cut me from the will, then later says what I've been saying all along, he cut me from the will after he received the letter.

He also says in answer to the CID's' question 28, "Is there any time that maybe"…and dad says "Never once have I exposed myself to her or any of the children", but the CID on reading out a part of C41 about our phone call, dads' reply to me was "All I done was got on top of you and *showed you what it was,* and I said that goes into mummy there" meaning my vagina. Which I'm sure was on the settee. He did expose himself, he got on top of me, (when he raped me). He said it himself.

My only route to getting justice, was blocked by the Crown Prosecution Service.

I then attempted suicide, and when that was stopped, I decided to appeal or seek a review through the CPS, which still didn't change their decision. So I thought I'd get my revenge on dad, but my anti-suicide drugs and all this writing, slowly but surely distanced me from murdering dad.

One day, I'm sure Karma *will* head for him.

The only time I feel my voice has been listened to and I can feel somewhat vindicated, since all the abuse happened, is when I was at the group, and able to say what I was ready to about what happened.

It then helped me when the statements and paperwork arrived here at my home in Wiltshire, I felt somewhat vindicated reading the questions that the CID asked when doing dad's' and the others' statements, and then when I included the statements into this book, me being able to finally say my piece in answer to them.

I'm not surprised at the gutless attitude of dad, with his programmed like saying of, 'Never, never whatsoever'. But at the end of the day they're all gutless.

STATEMENT THREE...

I will get round to the statement, which isn't much really but it needs this explanation first.

Approximately 1984, my Stepsister skived school one day in a tower block flat I lived in, in Kent. I'd written her a note for her teacher. Stepsister was lovely, and I thought we were going to get on ok.

We were in my kitchen, I was tidying a work top, whilst chatting. I eventually got around to asking her if she gets on alright with dad. She did. I told her if there were ever any problems, she's welcome to stay at my flat. I then went on to tell her about some of the sex abuse that I put up with for years.

She listened, then went quiet, then glared at me, then said "You bitch". I looked across at her and said "You what?" She then said "You slag", then "You cunt". I was confused and instantly getting wound up with her and said "Right, what's your problem, what have I done to deserve that?" She then said "You tart, you've got a really nice flat", but she was still glaring hard at me. I thought, 'Oh no, she's schizophrenic'.

I said "Right, I've done nothing wrong here, in fact I've helped you and offered to let you stay here if there were any problems at your house, and warned you about dad, and you've turned against me just like that, well you'd better go now before I put you out". She was gone and never came back.

A couple of years later, I'd got talking to dad in small doses. Approximately 1987, on a phone call from dad, he said "Yeah, when she (stepsister) went to your flat that time, she said something about me playing about with you, doing things to you, what was all that about?" I was about to blurt out "Well yes you did abuse me in the flats" but before I could say it, Rose took the phone off him and screeched at me saying "That wasn't your dad touching you, that was him telling you to change your knickers because your mum would let you wear the ones you wore to school, to bed aswell, then to bloody school again!". I felt humiliated, yet angry at the lie she screeched out at me about my mum, and angry at knowing dad lied to her about what he done to me. I yelled back at her, shouting "Well I was there every time, and I think I know what was going on more than you, you fucking witch!"

So that was those two with their lame attempt to make me believe I wasn't sexually abused.

I still felt I owed the stepsister that explanation about dads' behaviour, however, she still made a short statement in favour of dirty dad.

Statement three...

Not much here but she did say,

"Until last week, I have no recollection of Eliza ever talking to me about dads' behaviour towards her", and,

"I do not have any recollection of dad acting inappropriately towards Eliza, even as a child"

Well, the groping me in Broadoak Road in the kitchen, was right in front of her and Rose, and that day of skiving school at my flat was a myth then was it?

But at the end of the day, the brunt of the sex with dad, was before my Stepsister was born.

Complex – Post Traumatic Stress Disorder

IN STAGES, I'VE read the following, then copied and pasted the write up about Complex-Post Traumatic Stress Disorder. C-PTSD. I had Googled it and found a most interesting description about it from the 'Beauty After Bruises' website. I'm so glad to have permission to use this write up, which explains a lot more about me, than I can. Huge thank you's Beauty After Bruises.

It starts from here;

"It's likely you may already be familiar with PTSD. You may know it as the condition that affects war veterans and survivors of car accidents, natural disasters, and isolated acts of violence. Complex PTSD, however, is specific to severe, repetitive trauma that typically happens in childhood — most often abuse.

On the surface, it may seem like PTSD and Complex PTSD are none too dissimilar — they both come as the result of something deeply traumatic; they cause flashbacks, nightmares, and insomnia; and, they can make people live in fear even when they are safe. But at the very heart and center of C-PTSD - what causes it, how it manifests internally, the lifelong repercussions, and its ability to reshape a person's entire mind and outlook on life - is what makes it considerably different.

Complex PTSD at a Quick Glance

Complex PTSD comes as a response to multiple, prolonged traumas over the course of months or, more often, years. This can include emotional, physical, and/or sexual abuses; domestic violence; living in a war zone; being held in captivity; human trafficking and other organized rings of abuse. While there are exceptional circumstances where adults develop C-PTSD, it is most often seen in those who endured significant childhood trauma. For those who experience this in adulthood, being at the complete control of another human being (often unable to meet their most basic needs without them), coupled with there being no foreseeable end in sight, is what breaks down their psyche and affects them far more severely than the trauma alone. For those who go through this as children, the fact it occurs as the brain is still developing - particularly as that child is trying to learn who they are as an individual, understand the world around them, and build attachments to and relationships with others for the first time - alters the entire course of their psychologic and neurologic development. When an adult experiences a traumatic event, they have more tools to understand what is happening to them, their place as a victim of that trauma, and that they should seek support even if they don't want to. Children don't possess most of these skills or even the ability to separate themselves from another's unconscionable actions. The psychological and developmental implications of that become complexly woven and stitched into who that child becomes and believes themselves to be. ..all of which are much harder to untangle than the flashbacks, nightmares and other posttraumatic symptoms that often come later.

Another important thing to know is that the trauma to children resulting in C-PTSD (as well as dissociative disorders) is usually deeply interpersonal within that child's caregiving system. Separate from the traumatic events and the perpetrator, there is often an added component of neglect, hot-and-cold affections from a primary caregiver, or even invalidation of the trauma entirely to children who do try to tell someone they were being hurt. These mixed messages and conflicting attachments from those who are supposed to provide love, comfort and safety - all in the periphery of extreme trauma and developmental interruptions - create additional unique struggles that PTSD-sufferers alone don't always face.

To delineate some these hallmark challenges - as outlined in the proposed Complex PTSD criteria - we'll begin with the one that shows up the most often in day-to-day life: emotion regulation. Survivors with Complex PTSD have a very difficult time with emotions — experiencing them, controlling them and, for many, even just being able to understand or label them accurately. Many have unmanaged or persistent sadness, either explosive or inaccessible anger, and/or suicidal thoughts. They may be chronically numb, lack the appropriate affect in certain situations, or be unable to triage sudden changes in emotional content (or level out again after a great high/low). It's also very common for these survivors to re-experience emotions from trauma intrusively - particularly when triggered. These feelings are often disproportionate to the present situation, but are equal to the intensity of what was required of them at the time of a trauma — also known as an emotional flashback.

Difficulty with self-perception is another fundamental struggle for survivors whose identity development was so fiercely interrupted or heavily manipulated by someone with ulterior motives. In its simplest form, how they see themselves versus how the world perceives them can be fiercely different, beyond what is common or normal amongst the general public. Some may feel they carry or actually embody nothing but shame and shameful acts - that they are "bad". Others believe themselves to be fundamentally helpless; they were let down by so many who could've stopped their abuse but didn't, so it "must just be them". Many see themselves as responsible for what happened to them and thus unworthy of kindness or love because "they did this to themselves". An inexhaustible number of other survivors may feel defined by stigma, believe they are nothing more than their trauma, worry they are always in the way or an unforgivable burden, or sense they are just completely and utterly different from anyone or anything around them - that they are alien. Startling enough, all of these feelings and more can live inside someone whom, to you, seems like the most brilliant, competent, strong, and compassionate human being.

Interruptions in consciousness are also a common - and at times very scary - reality in C-PTSD. Some may forget traumatic events (even if they knew of them once before), relive them intrusively, recall traumatic material in a different chronological order, or experience other varying degrees of what is called dissociation. Dissociation is a symptom that exists on a spectrum and can range anywhere from more harmless forms like daydreaming or "spacing out"; to more disruptive experiences of feeling disconnected from one's body or mental processes, not feeling real, or losing time; all the way to the most severe, which includes switching between self-states (or alters, as is seen in Dissociative Identity Disorder). Episodes of missing time can range anywhere from a few minutes, a couple days, or even large chunks of one's childhood. The larger gaps in time are typically only seen in DID, but those with C-PTSD alone can still endure 'interruptions in consciousness' that result in memory gaps, poor recall, and traumatic material that is completely inaccessible (or, conversely, re-experienced against their will).

Difficulty with relationships may seem like a natural progression since each area mentioned so far can affect how fruitful your relationships are - but these challenges go well beyond a lack in quality or richness. This refers more to the potential to feel completely isolated from peers and not even knowing how to engage; harboring an outright refusal to trust anyone (or just not knowing why you'd ever want to); trusting people way too easily, including those who are dangerous, due to a dulled sense of alarm; perpetually searching for a chance to be rescued or to do the rescuing; seeking out friends and partners who are hurtful just because it feels familiar; or even abruptly abandoning relationships that are going well for any number of reasons.

With this in mind, and knowing more about the depths to which C-PTSD sufferers battle with their self-perception and interpersonal relationships, it may make it easier to empathize with them on the next category, which is:

The perception of one's perpetrators. This can be one of the most insidious battles for survivors with Complex PTSD — even if it seems crystal clear to those on the outside. Victims of such prolonged trauma may just eventually surrender, assuming their abuser(s) total power over them, possibly even maintaining this belief once they're 'free'. Others may feel deep sadness or profound guilt at just the thought of leaving them (including long after they've successfully left, if they were able).

Some may remain transfixed by their abuser's charming side or the warm public persona everyone loves, and can truly find it impossible to think ill of them. Many can hold a constant longing for their abusers to just love them - craving their praise well into adulthood, or slaving away in their personal lives just to make them proud. Alternatively, there are others who may obsess about them angrily, holding only hatred and disdain for them to the point of persistent bitterness and/or vengefulness. Some can even harbor desires to seek that revenge. (Though, it should be clearly noted that it is not at all common that they actually do; it's more about the thoughts than actions.) Many survivors can have a more primary, surface-layer set of thoughts/feelings about their abuser(s), particularly if asked. But it's helpful to understand that a collection of all these feelings and responses can (and often do) coexist within one person - vacillating between great extremes underneath that surface layer shown to the world. Day to day, and year to year, their feelings can shift - and - what the survivor knows to be true intellectually versus what they feel emotionally may remain incongruous for a very long time.

Of the many, many well-observed developmental disruptions those with C-PTSD face, one many find the toughest to conquer, even with therapy is one with which we very hope to offer help and support. That area is what's referred to as one's 'system of meanings' - one that, after being subjected to such tumultuous abuse as a child, it can be almost irreparably injured. What this criterion is referring to is how it may be impossible for them to hold on to any kind of sustaining faith, or belief there will ever be justice served to indiscretions of ethics or morality. Their outlook on life and the world at large can be unfairly contorted. They may doubt there is any good or kindness in the world that isn't selfish-hearted, or worry they'll never find forgiveness - possibly even believing they only came to this world to be hurt, so there can be no good coming for them. This level of hopelessness and despair, and these greater meanings assigned to their suffering, may also fluctuate greatly over time. There may even be periods of years where things no longer feel so bleak or as if they were conned of a meaningful life — only to wrestle with it again as more layers of their trauma are processed through and strike a chord inside of them. This is a common experience for so many survivors, with lasting ramifications, and we want to be here to help give pause to those deep swings into the darkness - doing what we can to help them stay in the light a little longer. Or, better yet, support them in putting some of that light inside of themselves. That way, even if they need to hide in the dark for a bit, it never leaves them for good. We're still here.

· Stay tuned for a page on Dissociative Disorders! For now, these two articles we've written provide a great introduction. Here and here! ·

WHY THEY NEED OUR HELP

There are less than 10 psychiatric hospitals in the US that offer specialized treatment for those with Complex PTSD and dissociative disorders. Other hospitals do not have the treatment teams or properly-trained unit staff needed to safely treat the nuances of complex trauma. Many are still sent to those facilities anyway.

Insurance providers prefer to work within their participating network of hospitals and therapists. Most will at least deny out-of-state care. With hospitals being in only a few states, this makes an inpatient admission an impossibility for many. For outpatient care, with treatment still both specialized and limited, searching for a participating provider within a given geographic area often yields zero results.

Without the participation of insurance, specialized hospitals are often forced to require up-front funding before accepting an admission. This funding can range anywhere from $10,000 to $50,000, and then accumulates once the patient stays beyond what that amount provides. Asking a patient to supply this astronomical fee while in a state of crisis and requiring a higher level of care, unsurprisingly, means many go without treatment.

Inpatient and intensive outpatient programs (IOP) for complex trauma are very grueling and comprehensive; they require longer-term stays to both stabilize patients and begin the therapeutic process. 3-6 weeks is an average length of stay for many programs, though some patients find they need care for a couple months or more once they've begun.

The lack of inpatient facilities and well-trained personnel isn't just a scarcity when it comes to higher levels of care. The number of outpatient therapists with the training and tools needed to treat Complex PTSD and dissociative disorders is shockingly low. The [falsely] perpetuated idea that therapists would never see cases like these, and the reality that clients who are suffering this way frequently struggle financially, keeps many professionals from making the time and financial commitment to further their education and become qualified clinicians.

Survivors with C-PTSD and dissociative disorders often require therapy for more than ten years on average. An additional number of years (up to several more) are all too often lost on ineffective or harmful therapy and receiving several misdiagnoses before ever obtaining a proper one. Following the most intensive phases of therapy, with memory processing completed, many patients still find themselves needing some form of therapy or psychiatric care for many, many years to come.

With a national average cost of specialized therapy sessions being $100 per visit, and clients often requiring twice weekly sessions for the first few years, out-of-pocket expenses can easily range from $5,000-$20,000 yearly. This does not include psychiatric care, medications, or the added travel expenses accumulated by those who must travel hour(s) to and from appointments.

Many insurance providers place a limit on the number of mental health-related expenses or appointments they'll cover yearly. This requires patients to either have a robust source of expendable income, or strategically plan and arrange their sessions like a puzzle just to gain what they can from their treatment before the days run out. Naturally, many lose access to the care they need and are forced to piece-meal their therapeutic journey in spurts each year, which is grossly ineffective.

A vast amount of patients with C-PTSD, and especially dissociative trauma disorders, can be so encumbered by flashbacks, dissociative symptoms, or other co-morbid physical/psychological disorders, they cannot work. This causes many to rely on state Medicaid programs which fail to provide skilled therapists trained in treating their condition. Medicaid programs also frequently fail to acknowledge the basic need for weekly visits, let alone more frequently or on an ongoing basis. The amount Medicaid is willing to reimburse a qualified therapist when negotiating a non-participating provider agreement, is often so minimal the therapists themselves cannot maintain a viable practice. They're forced to say no.

A More Complex Look At Complex Ptsd

The traumatic stress field has adopted the term "Complex Trauma" to describe the experience of multiple and/or chronic and prolonged, developmentally adverse traumatic events, most often of an interpersonal nature (e.g., sexual or physical abuse, war, community violence) and early-life onset. These exposures often occur within the child's caregiving system and include physical, emotional, and educational neglect and child maltreatment beginning in early childhood.
— Bessel A. van der Kolk

A Clinical Perspective: Including Co-Occuring Disorders And Trauma's Effects On Medical Health

COMPLEX POST TRAUMATIC STRESS DISORDER (C-PTSD) is a disorder that can result from severe, chronic, or extremely threatening trauma. Often, this trauma is also interpersonal, happens early in life, lasts for a long time, involves a mix of trauma types, or is followed by one or more unrelated traumas. C-PTSD involves all of the core symptoms of posttraumatic stress disorder (PTSD) in addition to symptoms that reflect the global impact of the trauma. Simply put, in addition to traumatic intrusions, avoidance, negative alterations in cognition and mood, and alterations in arousal and reactivity, C-PTSD also involves distorted perceptions of the victim's perpetrator (such as feeling positively towards an abuser, viewing them as all-powerful, or being obsessed with "getting even" with them), and the negative alterations in cognition and mood are much more extreme. For example, while someone with PTSD may feel depressed following a natural disaster, someone with C-PTSD may feel helpless, shameful, or completely different from other people following years of neglect or abuse. They may struggle to form interpersonal relationships and be caught between distrust and a need to escape feelings of isolation. They completely lose their faith and fail to find any meaning in life. As well, they may struggle with intense anger that they desperately try to inhibit or direct either outward in explosive bursts or inward through self harm or suicidal expressions. Finally, dissociation plays a far greater role in C-PTSD than it does in PTSD, and many individuals with C-PTSD struggle with chronic depersonalization (feeling like they are unreal) and/or derealization (feeling like the world around them is unreal), dissociative amnesia (being unable to remember some or all of the trauma), identity confusion (being unsure of who they are or feeling like the trauma destroyed their sense of self), or even identity alteration (switching between dissociative parts, or alters).

C-PTSD is very often comorbid with dissociative disorders, including dissociative identity disorder (DID) or other specified dissociative disorder (OSDD). Other common comorbidities include borderline personality disorder (BPD); depressive or bipolar disorders; anxiety disorders; obsessive compulsive disorders; eating disorders and substance abuse. Most individuals with DID or OSDD have C-PTSD because the trauma that caused their conditions was often interpersonal, chronic, and severe as well as something that occurred during childhood and so had a very strong developmental impact. In contrast, while C-PTSD is less common among individuals with BPD, BPD with comorbid PTSD shares many diagnostic features with C-PTSD - making it at times difficult to differentiate. Some key differences between the disorders are that the self harm or suicidal behaviors driven by emotional instability play less of a role in C-PTSD; individuals with just BPD have a shifting self concept whereas those with C-PTSD are seen to have a stable negative self concept; individuals with C-PTSD are more likely to feel isolated and distrustful rather than fearing abandonment and shifting between idealization and devaluation; and dissociation is more common in and plays a greater role in C-PTSD. Nonetheless, it is not at all uncommon for an individual to have both C-PTSD and BPD (or C-PTSD, BPD, and DID or OSDD) with some combination of other comorbid conditions. Again, this is because the type of trauma that can result in C-PTSD can have strong effects on an individual's relationships with others, relationship with their self, and even their ability to conceptualize themselves.

Where the negative symptoms of PTSD may be more temporary

or clearly understood to be a result of the disorder, individuals with C-PTSD may have their entire personalities and views of life shaped by their trauma history. Unfortunately, their symptoms aren't just limited to their mental state. Individuals with C-PTSD are also vulnerable to physical symptoms that cannot be medically explained but instead can be associated with their internal pain and stress. These physical symptoms, called somatic symptoms, can include neck and back pain; headaches and migraines; gastrointestinal problems including irritable bowel syndrome; allergies; thyroid and other endocrine disorders; chronic fatigue syndrome; or a disorder called fibromyalgia that involves widespread musculosketal pain, fatigue, and problems with sleep, memory, and mood. As well, the trauma that causes C-PTSD can trigger or exacerbate existing chronic illnesses or genetic vulnerabilities. All of this can push an already mentally and emotionally taxed trauma survivor past their limit when triggers increase their C-PTSD symptoms and cause their somatic or physical conditions to flare. In highly dissociative trauma survivors especially, such intense periods are likely to lead to emotional numbing, difficulties with autobiographical memory, periods of intense derealization or depersonalization, fugue episodes in which the individual travels and engages in actions while in a trance state, or switching between dissociative parts. While this can temporarily ease the pain of processing traumatic memories and physical ails, it can interfere with long term healing and make work, school, and interacting with others difficult. Dissociation as a response to the stress caused by trauma and resulting C-PTSD can also increase the risk of revictmization, or further trauma and abuse.

Sources:

---

http://www.ejpt.net/index.php/ejpt/article/view/25097

http://www.ptsd.va.gov/professional/PTSD-overview/complex-ptsd.asp

http://did-research.org/origin/comorbid/trauma-stress/c-ptsd.html

http://did-research.org/origin/comorbid/trauma-stress/ptsd.html

http://psychcentral.com/lib/complex-post-traumatic-stress-disorder/

http://www.healthyplace.com/blogs/understandingcombatptsd/2015/06/05/complex-posttraumatic-stress-disorder-ptsd-vs-simple-ptsd/

http://www.traumacenter.org/products/pdf_files/complex_ptsd.pdf

How I Relate To This Interesting Write Up.

YES IT IS very interesting to read almost all about myself by well knowledged survivors and other clever people.

From paragraph one C-PTSD At A Glance:

"For those who go through this as children, the fact it occurs as the brain is still developing - particularly as that child is trying to learn who they are as an individual, understand the world around them, and build attachments to and relationships with others for the first time - alters the entire course of their psychologic and neurologic development. When an adult experiences a traumatic event, they have more tools to understand what is happening to them, their place as a victim of that trauma, and that they should seek support even if they don't want to. Children don't possess most of these skills or even the ability to separate themselves from another's unconscionable actions. The psychological and developmental implications of that become complexly woven and stitched into who that child becomes and believes themselves to be. ..all of which are much harder to untangle than the flashbacks, nightmares and other posttraumatic symptoms that often come later"

As I said before, "I was inside this experience, living and learning it all at the age of five or six, (this sleeping and sex with my dad). I was often alone, and still am today apart from work. I don't socialise, and when in conversations during work, sometimes I can't reach others' flow, and gradually back out of conversations by looking busily into something (or nothing) on my phone. There's some stuff I just can't grasp. It's right to say all of which are much harder to untangle than the flashbacks etc. It's difficult seeing others of my age or even younger in full on conversation of a mature nature, which I almost feel embarrassed for not completing it with them because I can't match what they're on about. I've had the micky taken out of me in the past by the loud mouth in any group aiming their insults right at me, and I would've already lost track of what they were actually saying four sentences back. I'm drained and already gone into my own world. I can't reach some other level that others seem to be on.

FROM PARAGRAPH TWO C-PTSD AT A GLANCE

"Separate from the traumatic events and the perpetrator, there is often an added component of neglect, hot-and-cold affections from a primary caregiver, or even invalidation of the trauma entirely to children who do try to tell someone they were being hurt. These mixed messages and conflicting attachments from those who are supposed to provide love, comfort and safety - all in the periphery of extreme trauma and developmental interruptions - create additional unique struggles that PTSD-sufferers alone don't always face".

This piece took me back to the sheer despair and confusion when going to school with mine and dads' sex on my mind, then asking the morning playground supervisor where my Mum is and her sharp 'No' answer, and continuing through the school day mentally carrying the visions and smells and actual soreness and pains in my vagina, then the gut wrenching trauma of being at my aunts' front door looking for my Mum then being turned away by my aunt and my Mum, to be forced back to the flat with my dad for more sex with him. Suicide was already a seed in my head but the 'how to' wasn't there yet.

FROM PARAGRAPH THREE C-PTSD AT A GLANCE:

"Many have unmanaged or persistent sadness, either explosive or inaccessible anger, and/or suicidal thoughts. They may be chronically numb, lack the appropriate affect in certain situations, or be unable to triage sudden changes in emotional content (or level out again after a great high/low). It's also very common for these survivors to re-experience emotions from trauma intrusively - particularly when triggered. These feelings are often disproportionate to the present situation, but are equal to the intensity of what was required of them at the time of a trauma — also known as an emotional flashback."

As cheerful or bubbly as I probably show myself to be, there's like a base layer of ongoing depression. Along with this is the seething anger of the actual sex abuse that has yet to manifest. The suicide has been attempted once. Yes that anger is explosive as I feel it, and when it happens, it'll come out probably loud, blasphemous and pretty much childish because it's all I know how to feel. Sex with my dad is the reason for the anger. I have shouted at people years ago though, eg a road rage argument where the rage was actually pouring out from the sex abuse really. Anger's still within me.

From Paragraph Four C-Ptsd At A Glance:

"Some may feel they carry or actually embody nothing but shame and shameful acts - that they are "bad". Others believe themselves to be fundamentally helpless; they were let down by so many who could've stopped their abuse but didn't, so it "must just be them". Many see themselves as responsible for what happened to them and thus unworthy of kindness or love because "they did this to themselves". An inexhaustible number of other survivors may feel defined by stigma, believe they are nothing more than their trauma, worry they are always in the way or an unforgivable burden, or sense they are just completely and utterly different from anyone or anything around them - that they are alien. Startling enough, all of these feelings and more can live inside someone whom, to you, seems like the most brilliant, competent, strong, and compassionate human being."

Well I definitely didn't feel any shame this sex with dad and because it was with dad, I felt I wasn't doing anything wrong, however much I didn't want to do it, but I wasn't given a choice. Yes, I was fundamentally helpless and definitely let down by the youngest of my brothers who could've stopped the abuse but didn't. I do feel I'm different to many other people because of doing adult stuff with dad when I was five, and now I'm feeling like the most childish adult who can't grow out of it. Because I'm not a successful person, I do feel I'm nothing more than my trauma and been a right burden on my Daughter.

From Paragraph Five C-Ptsd At A Glance:

"Dissociation is a symptom that exists on a spectrum and can range anywhere from more harmless forms like daydreaming or "spacing out"; to more disruptive experiences of feeling disconnected from one's body or mental processes, not feeling real, or losing time; all the way to the most severe, which includes switching between self-states (or alters, as is seen in Dissociative Identity Disorder). Episodes of missing time can range anywhere from a few minutes, a couple days, or even large chunks of one's childhood."

I do realise when I've done that in the work place. The background sounds of the workplace goes quieter, whilst I'm flashing back to the two flats I was abused in. I don't recall leaving the real time or state, I just realise I've been 'away' at the flats for however long. I wrote in an earlier chapter about feeling like I'm back at the main flat I was abused in, and walking around as if I'm in the spirit world or behind a camera filming it. There are huge chunks of missing childhood aswell. What I've written about my childhood is basically all I can remember. There are large gaps of childhood times that have gone.

From Paragraph Six C-Ptsd At A Glance:

"Difficulty with relationships may seem like a natural progression since each area mentioned so far can affect how fruitful your relationships are - but these challenges go well beyond a lack in quality or richness. This refers more to the potential to feel completely isolated from peers and not even knowing how to engage; harboring an outright refusal to trust anyone (or just not knowing why you'd ever want to); trusting people way too easily, including those who are dangerous, due to a dulled sense of alarm; perpetually searching for a chance to be rescued or to do the rescuing; seeking out friends and partners who are hurtful just because it feels familiar; or even abruptly abandoning relationships that are going well for any number of reasons."

Yes, I don't socialise yet. I can't hold proper conversations, can't trust anyone, not just for relationships. I can't find trust in anyone in general. I've gone through several failed relationships mainly due to my lack of trust but this already lack of trust grew worse through relationships becoming violent, him playing away or I just got involved with a consistent liar. I once went camping with a guy and took my brother with us. For some weird reason I called it a day with this guy. As soon as we got back home, and my brother went back to his place, I was ok with my guy again. I don't have any idea why I dumped him temporarily then.

C-PTSD

"The perception of one's perpetrators. This can be one of the most insidious battles for survivors with Complex PTSD — even if it seems crystal clear to those on the outside. Victims of such prolonged trauma may just eventually surrender, assuming their abuser(s) total power over them, possibly even maintaining this belief once they're 'free'. Others may feel deep sadness or profound guilt at just the thought of leaving them (including long after they've successfully left, if they were able). Some may remain transfixed by their abuser's charming side or the warm public persona everyone loves, and can truly find it impossible to think ill of them. Many can hold a constant longing for their abusers to just love them - craving their praise well into adulthood, or slaving away in their personal lives just to make them proud. Alternatively, there are others who may obsess about them angrily, holding only hatred and disdain for them to the point of persistent bitterness and/ or vengefulness. Some can even harbor desires to seek that revenge. (Though, it should be clearly noted that it is not at all common that they actually do; it's more about the thoughts than actions.)"

Over the abusive years, I went back to dad because I had to look up to him because he's dad. I did want proper praise about anything like school work etc but I only got favouritism when being told it's 'our secret.' I explained it as best as I could in my chapter 'It's A Bit Like

Stockholm Syndrome'. Even when we'd got Mum back and moved to Kent, if dad visited us, I'd still look up to him and show respect. These days, now it's all in the open, I could easily kill the bastard. Planning revenge was what got me to sleep at night but I don't want him dead yet. He has to have a copy of my book first!

C-PTSD:

"Of the many, many well-observed developmental disruptions those with C-PTSD face, one many find the toughest to conquer, even with therapy is one with which we very hope to offer help and support. That area is what's referred to as one's 'system of meanings' - one that, after being subjected to such tumultuous abuse as a child, it can be almost irreparably injured. What this criterion is referring to is how it may be impossible for them to hold on to any kind of sustaining faith, or belief there will ever be justice served to indiscretions of ethics or morality. Their outlook on life and the world at large can be unfairly contorted. They may doubt there is any good or kindness in the world that isn't selfish-hearted, or worry they'll never find forgiveness - possibly even believing they only came to this world to be hurt, so there can be no good coming for them."

True. I'll never get over the cancelled trial, no justice served. I do know there are many kind people on this planet. I don't get why I don't meet them. I definitely won't forgive my nonce, and I do seem to run into those relationships that end up with me being hurt and don't seem to have much good coming for me, apart from a beautiful Daughter. (Whose father I divorced within a year of meeting him, because of consistent lies, so the trust was lost).

I think Beauty After Bruises have done a really well explained write up about C-PTSD. I can relate to most of it. I bet others with the same diagnosis can recognise a lot of it in their lives. I believe that anyone who has suffered childhood sex abuse, who hasn't spoken out about it to anyone, should go and be listened to for their own sake, not necessarily to take their abuser to court because justice doesn't always happen, and that same lack of justice sent me insanely revengeful. Once I'd first been listened to by The group (here in the UK) back in the '90's, I felt relief that someone believed me that multiple abuse/rapes happen. It was autonomous for me to deal with each incident at a time and one resurfaced horrific memory. I know many haven't been through as much as I have, and sadly many have been through more prolonged, worse abuse. I still want to be listened to by a professional even now. Being listened to was the right therapy whilst being believed. The professionals are alongside the victims/survivors, they know our horrors of childhood. They are resilient, gentle and completely understanding. I don't know if I'd be here now if I hadn't been listened to in the '90's for the first time. Being listened to and writing my thoughts down made a load of difference. I couldn't have held on to the abuse all by myself, and I wish I'd sought that help many years before I did.

"The Group West Wiltshire

The group is Wiltshire's Rape, And Sexual Abuse Centre (RASAC). It's where counselling and caring, meaningfully goes on.

It's in a peaceful building set in a bustling town in Wiltshire.

In that peaceful place, there are friendly faces of people who do care, very much actually. They have a knowing look with their warm welcome, and they truly connect without judging you. They take hold of your experiences as you deal with the impact those experiences have on you, and fully support you on your journey forward.

What a moment when I met for the first time, a well-knowledged woman… It was the knowing look on her face, which felt like a spiritual moment. I'd never met her before, yet it was like she knew me.

Back in 1999 to 2000, when I was 39 years old, she welcomed me in to The group, where I had an initial meeting with her before she introduced me to my counsellor. It was where all the sex abuse and other incidents that had gone on in my life, was finally, properly, spoken about to a professional for the first time.

Initially, I was worried about the stuff I needed to say, would prompt them to call the police, because I wasn't ready for all that. I remember mentioning several times, "This won't end up in court will it?" I was gently assured that no one's calling the police and my appointments will be confidential and all about *my* healing.

In the introduction meeting with Annie, I explained my experiences in a rapid, full speed blurt like I do, quite often actually. I don't stop for breath when there's so much to say to someone I completely trust. When I had made a gap for her to speak, she clarified, expertly deciphered, what I'd spluttered out beforehand, then she would go to say something, as if she's read my mind and set me off into another rant after butting in on what she's trying to say. She didn't flinch, tutt or react in any way about me butting in. I couldn't stop myself rambling on. It had been with me all my child and adulthood, and I'd finally started to spill. My sick historical's were rolling out.

She did get a few sentences across to me, eventually. She definitely knew the pain, shock and stress I'd been suffering as a result of the abuse. She knew my past as if she'd experienced the same pain and sabotaged childhood. She doesn't only listen. She feels it. She felt that pain with me, tch it's quite sad in the way that she can truly know me from what's gone on, all because it *might've* been her past too. There's me waffling away like billy-O, all about me, like I'm the only one on the planet who's been sexually abused and raped, by their sad excuse of a dad, and I suddenly think like, 'Well who listens to all the counsellors of this world?'. She really had the full understanding of the whole of my life up to those counselling sessions and she meant it when she said "We'll walk alongside you", and she did, with my counsellor for the following six months.

Throughout my counselling sessions with the equally caring listener, I'd often taken in drawings and writings of the nightmares I'd suffered about dad abusing me, and of him following me, or further nightmares of dad sleeping with me. We'd talk them through in the sessions after they'd happened, then later in each session, have a resting of minds moment, where we sat with our eyes closed and visualised anything peaceful for five or ten minutes, then talk of hopes of going forwards. After each counselling session, I begun to feel saved. By the next session, I was well in need of her help again.

When I suffered that resurfaced memory amongst that nightmare. For once, I could hardly speak to any counsellor. I was stuck with shock. I did eventually get it over to one of them during that counselling session, all be it in fragmented sentences.

More of this disgusting crime committed by dad was hitting my head in waves as I recalled the sick experiences. I told her the rawness of the visions as they erupted. Eg: "Dad was blowing raspberries on my groin". Moments later, "My dress is pushed up" "He was licking me", then a moments' silent pause, then, "Dad done oral sex on me". That was my re-surfaced memory.

The nightmare part of it was all of that, but instead of me, it was India who dad was approaching to do that on. She was a toddler, and she was laid down on the sideboard behind that settee where he actually done it to me.

Trying to explain all that whilst in shock, and knowing it was a resurfaced memory, was really painful to manage, even to the most trusting listener. Then the nightmare side of it happening to India, immediately erupted so much anger into me that I envisaged me swinging a cricket bat, hard into dads' head, with his blood splattered everywhere, then seeing dad pleading me to stop. He can plead the fuck on, 'til he can plead no more.

I know I was mentally 'done in' by his actions. This shock and anger went on for over a week. It was flashback, flashback flashback, one straight after the other of the feelings of him touching me, on my wet groin and vagina. Then it was of the sounds of his raspberry blowing on me, and his stupid childish talk and the smokey/nicotiney stench, and that urgent moment in the nightmare where I needed to scream out to India to warn her to get up and run to me.

All those visions, sounds and smells, where being re-enacted as each flashback hit me. I hardly spoke to my own Daughter for a week, all because of the stressful disorder, created by dads' noncing upon me.

I dread to think what I'll do if another memory resurfaces of his noncing upon me. I doubt the police will get a look in next time, well, what's the point? Where did it all get me after all that stuff gone on?

Back in the counselling session, when all that could be said, was done so, and the resting of minds after. I didn't want to leave the tranquil sanctuary in that large old building I just wanted to go into a darker room in that building and cry, and only yell out to one of them of my realisation and anger of dads' oral sex upon me, but even if I could've done that, the right words wouldn't come fluently to mind, thanks to the shock from it. My mind was lost from all order and routine, apart from the mothering instinct. Locking myself in a dark room, yelling out my feelings and bawling my eyes out would've felt good, but I couldn't cry even if someone paid me to, and more importantly, I had the sweetest little six year old, my India, to collect from school.

The group helped me start the ball rolling to de-congest my mind of the years of dads' sex abuse, revenge and suicidal thoughts, and with their help and support, I was able to engage my mind towards the start of this book.

Obviously, over the years since, there's been many thousands more flashbacks and another resurfaced memory of the attempted or successful rape by dad, which all reloaded my head again, and led to the reporting it to Wiltshire Police, with that and the CPS, and then the suicide attempt, I needed to start writing again.

I made a random appointment with the group in June '16. It was a suggestion on an MHT counsellors' letter, confirming a one off appointment we had, about anxiety I suffer, and my wish of the bloody flashbacks to go away. He'd mentioned about me talking to the group again, so I thought I'd take him up on that suggestion, and glad I did.

I met the one in charge almost straight away. She doesn't forget a face nor an incident and she hasn't changed a bit, and straight away, she asked how India is doing, like it was only about a month since I'd last seen her.

Well I still ranted a lot and butted in a hell of a lot, and I still learned from her.

For years, I've thought about having hypnosis, hoping to alleviate me of flashbacks. I asked her if there are any hypnotists about and can they do that. Because I'm thinking; If I moved to an area and home I want, and got four grandchildren from India, and got the two dogs, two cats and chickens, and everything's right in my life. I'll probably still keep flashing back won't I, because my childhood experiences are always there in my head. She opened my eyes, when she explained the downside of me having hypnosis, which I'd never thought about, that it can also resurface more memories of sex abuse which may have been surpressed. I didn't anticipate that, and even though I don't know what to do to rid me of these flashbacks, I can't be sure I haven't supressed any more of dads' sex abuse. I also know, if I'm put through that type of shock from any resurfaced memory ever again, I won't trust the CPS or go through all that lawful side of life again, oh no!, Not on top of a resurfaced memory. There's only one satisfactory solution left that will justify how I'll feel from what dad done to me.

Survivors of sex abuse and rapes, can move forward and live a full proper life. I still struggle to turn my life round to that at the moment. I like to think it'll happen to me once I can get this published. At the moment, words like "Don't let him win" "Don't let him still have a hold on you" etc etc, are still just *words,* they don't actually mean anything in my head right now.

Knowing The group will be beside me whenever I need them, really cushions the blow..

"The Criminal Injuries Compensation Authority (Cica).

ON MY WAY out from the Police interview in a Wiltshire Police Station, the Duty Solicitor advised me I could make a claim for Criminal Injuries from the Criminal Injuries Compensation Authority (CICA). I told him I believe I couldn't, because the trial was cancelled. He explained that I can because it's not paid by the perpetrator.

I gave it a week or so before looking into it. I felt I had nothing to lose, and filled an online form in. I found it helpful telling someone all that had happened, clearly in writing, so it was a bit of therapy if nothing else.

I received their response to my claim in mid-May 2015. I was turned down for an award because "Under Paragraph 19 of The Scheme, an award will not be made in respect of a criminal injury sustained before 1 October 1979 if, at the time of the incident giving rise to that injury, the applicant and the assailant were living together as members of the same family".

So, let me get this right. I'm not entitled to compensation for the sex abuse by my dad because I was living with him, right?

I know I didn't ask to be sexually abused, but what!? What!? Should I have let all that keep happening the way it did, then sleep wherever else? Is that the expected scenario required in order to award victims of sex abuse, compensation?

I was left at the flat by my mum, she was back for a while, then gone again, then I found her, then she forced me back to the flat, which forced me to live with dad there and Rose's flat. I couldn't do anything to escape him. Those stories he told me of the spooks of the night outdoors, I believed, so couldn't just run off, because I was too scared. When we were at the flat, he abused me. When we were at Rose's flat, he abused me, and when we were at his and Rose's' house, he abused me.

Mum didn't want me then, and I had no choices like youngsters have these days when one can call Childline, or confide in a trusted relative or teacher. With no phone, no relations around, and scared to mention it to anyone in school, because it's "our secret". I had not even one choice.

I called CICA, expressing my confusion at this "Scheme", asking the guy, "What was I meant to do?" Obviously, he couldn't change this rule, but advised me to appeal within a certain time, which I did.

Meanwhile, my thoughts were thrown from seriously not bothering to try and claim criminal injuries, to "but it's me again, no justice or acknowledgement" I've not lied about any of this. I simply wanted justice and acknowledgement. Compensation wasn't on my mind during all this court stuff or later on, during the caution. I'd heard about it, but didn't think of it in relation to me because of, and whilst being, hell-bent on revenge.

So after further thought, I decided to not let myself endure a whole new heap of legal complexities, like my fight against the cps and decided a solicitor should be able to help me on this one, I mean a solicitor who might know about this "Scheme", because the duty Solicitor didn't seem to know about it. So I contacted one, who couldn't help, then another, and another, then Ward Councillor, local MP, and heck! I was on another wave of knockbacks for seeking help, and getting nowhere fast *just like* the cps fight all over again.

One solicitor kindly explained in his email reply, about the domestic violence victims who went back to their partners after receiving compensation, then the partners benefitting from the proceeds. I started receiving other replies from those I sought help from but they were all rejections to my needs, and they're all too complex for my skull, then to be able to write it clearly here.

Within my appeal, or application for a review, I put;

"I do not accept your decision, which is based on "The Scheme" mentioning Paragraph19. I am lead to understand, by a Solicitor, that "The Scheme" and/or paragraph 19 was designed to prevent 'battered wives' claiming compensation for assaults by their husbands, and then getting back together with them, with the husbands benefitting from the proceeds.

This discriminates against people like myself, who suffered historical sexual abuse.

My Mother had gone away. I wasn't allowed to go with her. I was forced, at the age of 4 or 5, to live with my 'dad', who was my abuser.

My case is a world away from a grown woman fleeing domestic violence, claiming, then returning to the partner. It's nothing like being sexually abused throughout childhood, with no choice to leave.

Can you please separate the domestic violence rule, from the childhood sexual abuse, and compensate abuse victims for life long PTSD, anger, depression, suicide attempts and ruined relationships, and allow us to find fulfilment of how life should be, and move on, away from this darkness?

I have contacted my MP with the same details, with hope of stopping this discrimination against adult survivors of historical sex abuse, thank you.

I went ahead and asked for a review, adding the fact that I had no escape from my abuser.

CICA replied saying 'It's not to do with domestic violence victims, I was ill-advised, again, by another Solicitor.

Here I am once again, in the midst of another fight, for acknowledgement and now compensation for my turbulent childhood.

I initially thought, "Y'know what, bollocks to it! To my childhood, and English justice!".

I'd had enough of this lack of justice, pathetic decisions and perverted liars driving me to the brink of suicide, and now realise I'm never going to afford a Solicitor to help me and don't seem to be able to find one who knows about The Scheme anyway.

I can't keep writing this book, emailing and phoning Solicitors, MP's, all and sundry. I had to stop somewhere. The Solicitors who *did* get back to me, told me they cannot help with this matter and/or haven't got the funding.

Then I remembered...Writing this book is stopping me from murdering my nonce, It's been stopping me from committing suicide, and this appeal to the CICA, isn't just about me. It's a tiny bit of probably thousands of us victims of sex abuse, rejected for compensation because of "The Scheme", which is a rule.

Rules can be changed.

So I continued to apply for a review.

"My grounds for appealing are;

Yes, I was living with my assailant as a member of the same family at the time of the incidents and before 1/October/1979, I understand that. To me, it's just a rule, and rules can be changed. Also to me, it's a major part of my life, a time of innocence and the vital learning years into my teens, swiped out of my life.

At the time of the abusive years, my mother had cleared off and told me she didn't want me with her, and told me I had to stay with my 'dad'. I was four years old when she told me that and left us. Four years old, and no choices, and was <u>forced to live with my sex abuser.</u>

He abused me all the time I had to live with him, and when my mother came back, and I had to sometimes go to the flat that he'd cleared off to with my mothers' .best friend, he took me to bed to make me sexually satisfy him, whilst Rose was in the living room. And at their new house later years."

So that was my appeal which I sent with the completed form required within it.

I tried to get my Solicitor to help me. He didn't realise about The Scheme, and offered no further help. I emailed someone at a university via a link about The Scheme, to ask if they knew about The Scheme but he didn't get back to me.

I tried the Ministry of Justice, who if I remember correctly were the people who told me to appeal to the CICA, which I had already done, so after all the searching for a knowledged somebodys' help and getting nowhere, the appeal I done actually lead to a first tier appeal, which brought a tribunal in Bristol Law Courts, February 2016.

In February 2016 I drove to a local Wiltshire coach park, paid to park up for the day then received a call from the court seconds before I boarded the coach for Bristol. The court woman apologised, saying the case has been adjourned because someone who's been through all the steps I and many others have been through, has managed to get this fight to the High Court. It's July 2018 now. This case is stayed

167

So, as usual, everything to get justice, has become a fight. I am waiting to hear from the CICA from the High Court now.

September 2018, I heard on the news, that the case is starting and I believe it'll run into 2019. Let's hope every victim within this rule, gets well compensated and that chance to move away from all this.

The Other Perpetrators

A Freak From Dartford.

We'd met when I was walking to school. He was a labourer at the new office building site in a place called Kent. We met up one evening, down a road parallel to my road, and we chatted, then a while later, kissed, and he told me to stand up, because we'd been sitting at the steps, in a local Road, where all us locals used to hang out. He made me lean my back against the fence of the gardens, which lined the alleyway running back from the steps, and as we were kissing, with my coat open and around him aswell, he actually tried getting it on with me. In a bloody alleyway for christs' sake. I wasn't tempted, nor going for it in a bloody alley and near home.

He did meet me again another day. We walked around an old local market one Saturday. It was where the Orchard Theatre is now. We'd done a few rows of stalls, when he led me away to the side of the market rows, at the back of some buildings. There was a three sided wall about four feet high, which surrounded steps, going down into darkness, which turned right at the end, I had no idea why we were really there, I thought we'd be getting up no good in some sort of burglary sense, because of there being a door there, which you could just see. The next thing, he kissed me, hugging me, then I had a lump of glass or jagged metal pushed against my throat, and he forced me to give him oral sex. He said, "If you don't get down there and suck it, you'll get this!" I think I was about 15 at the time, and I said, "No! I'm not doing that!" It's true, that I wasn't actually frightened. I was a bit upset, gutted and annoyed because of the way he's treating me, and really didn't know if he would've done it, but I had no way out of there because he blocked me.

THE RAPIST FROM SOUTH LONDON

I was 12 or 13 years old. 1973, and hanging out with 3 mates on the green in our local area, it was a set back row of houses, with public footpath round the perimeter of 2 fenced off grassed areas, (chain link fence). We were chatting away, when J arrived. I had quite liked him, he was one of the older guys, at our school, and brother of my friend. He joined in conversation, and it wasn't unusual for me to bring the subject up about motorbikes, talking about the dream bike to own etc. He said he's got posters of chopped bikes in his room, from bike magazines. I wanted to see them, he wanted to show us them, so we all upped and went, through an alley, and across to his house.

We went up the stairs, and I knew where his bedroom was because of being in there before, when his sister, my friend, wanted to snoop around.

True enough, he had posters and centre pages of chopped bikes up on his wall, which I don't remember seeing on mine and his sisters' snooping missions. His bed was on the right, along the side wall of the house, under a window. I can't now remember what else was in the room. We'd looked at the posters and started making our way out of his room.

Myself and the other girls were just outside the door, when J grabbed me, pulled me back through the door. I told him to get off me. The other girls pushed the door but he pushed them back and shut the door by leaning on it to stop them forcing it open. I was also trying to get out at the same time. He had a small sliding bolt on it and locked it with that. He pushed me onto his bed, and I was instantly trying to get back up again, but his strength was more than mine. He was tugging my underwear down, whilst I was still struggling, trying to keep them on and stop what he was doing, and telling him to 'fucking get off me!" but his strength got the better of me, and raped me. He actually had the gall to say sorry after that. I remember leaving that room snivelling, shocked, and angry. I got up the road to my house, and as soon as I walked in, I said to my mum, "That fucking bastard J made me have it with him!". I told her who I was talking about, but nothing was done about it.

I'm still sure those friends who witnessed that, remember it.

CROSS DRESSING INEPT ONE FROM WILTSHIRE.

I'd not long moved into our first 2 bed house in Wiltshire, I had some guy booked to connect appliances for me. He turned up and it wasn't long before he asked me out. I really wasn't sure because I was new to the area and didn't know anything about him, but was in need of company.

We started seeing each other and he really did have a weird character, which was eccentric to put it politely. No top front teeth, he was a cross dresser, plays a guitar and sings…but couldn't play the guitar, or sing if his life depended on it, get my drift?

One of those balmy days, we ended up in bed, with the idea of sleeping. He was really getting agitated though, he was getting touchy feely, which made me think, what's the point of going to bed, to sleep, if I can't be allowed to?

It was the same old crap you get from disrespectful types, he was pushing into me with a boner, which made me less want to have it, than I already didn't. He got on top of me, I told him to get off me. He was like something possessed, pretty scary. He did end up raping me, then he went asleep. The following morning in the kitchen, I stood by the cutlery drawer for easy access to a knife if it came to it I told him "That was the first, and last time you ever do that to me. Try it again, and someone else will help me deal with you, and I don't mean the Police" He made some pathetic excuse, something about thought I was up for games like that. If it wasn't for India, being so young, and only me to depend on, I think I would've sought revenge on him.

Remember. Multiple abuse and rapes really happens. As I said in the beginning, about when you've learned to say "No", a perpetrator rarely listens to what you want. It's all about what they want and usually, forcefully get.

When all these perverts turn up in my head, one after the other or the whole incident by one, I do want to end it all. However, thoughts of revenge, planning revenge and mentally acting it out, usually helps me sleep whilst thinking about the result.

An Uncle From Kent..

I used to belong to the local District Swimming Club for several years, and went on to do life-saving training, when I was 14. My cousins followed suit, which was expected, but it was handy because I got a lift off my uncle every week. Mum & I were seeing more of him at our house, which I was alright about because we rarely saw men in the house since both bro's moved out.

He was Scottish, short, nearly bald and round. It was nice to get his attention though. I thought he and Mum were seeing each other at one point because he kept turning up so often.

One particular day, he arrived again, without my cousins. We'd begun chatting, when mum popped out of the room. She'd taken some time, and still out of the room, when he started talking about me. Telling me I'm good looking, thick hair etc, basically sweetening me up, without me realising. I'd said to him "No, I've got a big spot, and don't like it". He said "No you haven't. Where?. I told him on my chin (or forehead, can't remember). He said "I can't see any spot, move closer, I might be able to see it then", which I stupidly, well, innocently did.

I was nearly against the settee between his shins to show him, when he grabbed my breasts. I said "What are ya doing?" He said "Ah come on, just one handful, they're beautiful, your mum won't find out". I said "Get off!", whilst pulling away from him. I didn't know which way to turn, what to say next or how to look at him or mum again. I was probably bright red after that because I felt the heat on my face. Mum came back in and I looked at her as if to say 'Get him out of here, now!" I feared creating a scene there and then, I didn't think about the word perv', I don't think I'd heard of that word then, but I did feel like punching him in the face and screaming "Fuck off out!", but me being me, had to shut my thoughts and actions away again, and accept another dirty bastard groped me.

I wasn't looking forward to the following Sunday morning, so on the following Saturday, whilst playing on a rope swing by the river, in a lane locally to us, I told Lynn, a class mate with me, about what happened, and that I'm not going back home.

There was an overgrown track, which lead to the rope swing, about 100 metres from the road. The river was to the left, and further ahead down the track, was a dip, with a length of corrugated metal over it. I decided to stay there that night, hoping I'd be brave as it got darker. Eventually Lynn had to go home for the night, and I settled down in my 'shelter'. I was thinking back on conversations about Lynn bringing a school dinner doggy bag down to me the following day, and dropping some biscuits etc off to me from her home earlier on, had some fags and matches too. I was comfortable for the night, but a bit scared, but I'd rather be there than having R grabbing me again potentially again the following morning.

I was hearing some wildlife sounds, probably for about an hour, when I heard Lynn calling me, I met her, with her Dad, which was no problem, because him, her mum and sisters, are one of the genuine, loveliest families I'd ever met. I'd already met them all and had sleepovers there. Her Dad would often make me roll up laughing because I have dimples in my cheeks when I laugh or smile. He used to say "Can I put my tongue in your dimples", and walk up to me. I didn't find anything wrong with that, I saw that as genuinely funny, all of us did. The whole family are great and caring.

Lynn had explained what I'd experienced from R, and of my plan to sleep in the shelter that night. She was worried about me being out there alone. We walked back to Lynns' house, and I had a bath and was allowed to stay the night there. Lynns' Dad spoke to my Mum about my uncles' actions. The following day, I went home and Mum said "Don't worry, he won't be coming back here". There was no police intervention.

He eventually got divorced then cleared off to Canada, with some other woman, where he died. One down! And outta my life!

FAT BASTARD CAB DRIVER

I was a despatch rider for a local taxi firm

On one of my more skint days, I'd be worrying whether I'd be able to travel home and manage to get back into work to get petrol allowance subbed to me. This worry happened far too often.

My 250 US Custom Yamaha, was gradually getting wrecked, due to this job. I was thinking of looking for another job anyway. The bike had gone on reserve, which means all the petrol in the tank had been used, except the small reserved amount once I'd turned a tap round under the tank. Not good, because I'd probably get home but not back into work again the following morning.

Everyone got along together, cabbies and riders alike, often telling each other funny passenger and customer moments, and at the other end of the scale, we'd look out for each other if any problems with customers etc. We were all at one in that little office.

I asked if any of the riders or drivers were heading in the same direction as me. After about 5 minutes and a few yells on the radios, one driver was found, who could get me all the way home. With the day's runs complete, the cabbie was ready to take me home.

We left South London and made our way towards Kent. Along the dual carriageway, he said he wanted to stop for a wee, and pulled over in a layby, which had a screen of trees between there and the main road. I can't remember anything of conversation we had, but there was a mention of my breasts, which I played down… uninterested.

He told me to kiss him, I said no, thinking, what the hell do I want to kiss him for? He leant towards me and said "Come on", and he pulled my head closer to him, forcing our lips to touch, and he pulled my hand onto the boner he had. I strained to pull away from him but the size and strength of him overpowered me. He then said "Get your mouth on it", I said "No! I want to go home". "Come on, just do it, get your mouth round this, then I'll take you home" he said. The selfish bastard, wasn't hearing me, he just wanted his satisfaction.

I managed to pull away but as I done so, he pulled me onto him, and forced me to do the full oral on him. He was a fat pervert, with a face like a pig. I was unable to break from his grasp, and walk the next 3 or so miles into Kent in the dark. He drove me home, whilst I was full of hatred towards this fat gutted slob, and I got out of his car, saying nothing out loud to him, because of the neighbours, but under my breath, I called him a 'dirty bastard', and I was shocked about more forced sex upon me. I do hope he's dead now too, the fat headed bastard!

V ERITH

I was living on the 12th floor of a tower block on the edge of South London with my then 18month old Daughter India. I'd done an application for a house, to get us on the list sooner rather than later. There was no 'Choice based lettings' service for bidding in those days. It was a case of keep phoning them up or write to them.

Indias' bedroom was a play room by day, a very colourful one too.

After getting some toys, and a plastic table, for her, I'd popped them into her room, and let her play with them. I was in the living room, when I suddenly heard one of her Leprechauns playing its' tune, thinking it had been blown down from her window sill by the breeze.

The window was open on the first setting, which had no actual open gap, it was on the latch on the outside edge of the window frame width open, and the sill was a good 4 to 5ft up from the floor. So I was sure all was safe, with the knowledge she was chatting away to her teddies and dolls.

I went into her room to put her Leprechaun back on the window sill, 'knowing' there's no way India could reach that window. I had a blind panic on entering her room because she'd upturned her plastic table, managed to climb up onto it. She was still on the table, yet leaning over the front edge of the window sill. Her Leprechaun was still up there, and she was on her way back down after playing with it, we had to press it's tummy to activate it. Had it have dropped onto it's tummy, it was possible to activate the tune on it, which is why I thought that's what had happened. That was far too risky and it wasn't going to happen again, and my determination to get out of that flat and into a house was paramount.

After getting nowhere, with the council, I sought help from a Ward counsellor. I was initially palmed off by a couple of people in that line of work, so I nagged away at them, and they told me V was going to visit me the following day, which was a Sunday.

I let him in, and lead him to my bedroom, which was a temporary living room because I was decorating the proper living room. We chatted away about his health, the RAF, procedures for the housing list, and….my legs. Yes, he said "What a lovely pair of 'pins' you have".

'Yeah?" I thought, whilst trying to talk about something, anything else, like housing? not my bloody legs.

We finally went through some of the relevant conversation, then an elderly woman knocked at my front door. I just looked at her, thinking she's gotta be at the wrong door, I don't even know her. She said "Oh I think I saw 'v ******' coming into your flat did I, what is he doing there?". I said "What?" Thinking 'is this on camera or something?' He heard her say it, and came to the door. I heard him say "What do you want, I'm visiting someone who needs my help!". I walked off and made a cuppa, thinking 'What the fuck is going on here?' He got back from Mrs nosey, and we completed the reason he visited, then he said he'd call back to update me about help with housing.

Some days after, he turned up without phoning me, I wasn't expecting him, but hey, let him in because he might have some update for me. Back in the room we were in before, and he started talking about no answer yet from housing, but we agreed to go up there together to put my case across and hopefully get a house. Or lower floor at least. I'd made it clear that I'm not going to private rent because I was unable to afford it. So there we were, still waiting for them to get back to him, so why didn't he phone me to tell me that?

He was about to leave, and he stood up from the armchair, came across to me, and handed to me a pound for India, and a pair of tights for me, telling me to "Put them on your lovely pins"

I offered them back, telling him with a nervous giggle "Me? Tights? I don't wear tights, I'm always in jeans, thanks anyway". He told me I should put them on. I do believe he meant, put them on there and then and let him see me with them on because he was just 'loitering' in the hallway by my kitchen, where I'd bunged the tights. This guy was becoming more wierd with each breath I took!

He rang me a couple of days later, giving me an appointment time to be up at the council offices, where we met a housing officer, and put it to her about the few dangers around the flat and an aggressive neighbour having a go at me in the lift etc. Up until this point, v had said nothing, not a word, I'd done all the talking so far. Then v says to me "Have you not considered renting privately?" This has to be a joke init! I glared at him, looked at the housing officer in what must've been a stunned expression on my face. We left there knowing that visit was a total waste of time.

Another day or so later, he turned up again uninvited, and hadn't phoned me before. I asked why he was here, hoping he'd say, he's got news about my housing application. He told me he wants to talk. Ok, I let him in. He talked, I wondered, and wondered, when the hell he was going to talk about my housing case, because so far, he'd been rabbiting on about my pins, and anything else but housing.

I was stood, leaning against the window sill. India was on the settee to my right, and he was in the armchair in front of me to my left. He stood up, making me think he was going to leave, so I, with great relief, moved forward, to show him to the door, thinking, 'yes! No more creepy talk of tights etc'

He didn't turn round to the door, he moved towards me, raising his arms, then clasped his hands onto my upper arms, and kissed me. I backed away a bit, then said "What are you doing!?" He replied, "I hope you don't mind me doing that?", whilst lightly lowering his right arm down from near my left shoulder, and very lightly stroked my left breast.

India's little face, saddened immediately. I imagine my face was glaring at him. My thoughts were raging. He turned away from me, and started making his way towards the bedroom door, then the front door. In that short distance, I'd visualised punching him in the back, basically beating the fuck out of him. India being there, and v mentioning a health scare to do with his heart, was all that stopped me retaliating. He turned around and said "I trust this will all be kept quiet". I made it clear that "I'm not that kind of woman, and you'd better go…Now!"

He was a proper weird one, who, after having him cautioned by the Police, I learned much more about him. He'd wanted to be in the running to become the Mayor, but after the cautioning, there was an 11th hour meeting, which brought an end to him being voted for it.

It was in the local paper about this incident. My aunt, a week or so later, phoned me to say, "I bought you SOME TIGHTS!" (she raised her voice when she said 'some tights') for India, but they'll be a bit long now".

She, with another aunt, came up to the flat. I did let them in the living room. They didn't smile, they looked seriously at India. They questioned, or rather, they lectured me about V being not like that.

They came to speak total bullshit about the incident, which they didn't know the facts about. Why? because they help out during canvassing time for local elections, for the same party as him.

After they left, those nearly 3.5 foot long tights went straight down the chute. They really was not happy with me because of reporting that perv to the Police. Just like dad. People like those two, and my 'family', would rather call their own flesh and blood a bloody liar, rather than protect them, just to save face of the perv's.

There was a full front page on this story in the local Times paper. Some other parties, expressed their thoughts on it, even one saying he was eccentric. Tell me about it! A few weeks after that, he was hospitalised and later died, and all those in office, who slated/slagged him off, earlier, were suddenly jumping on the same bandwagon, being full of praise for him. I gave as good as I got in the local paper.

I was even accused by his wife, of murdering him in 'her side of the story' in the local paper. She really couldn't have known him well, and…she wasn't even there when it happened! There was a photograph of the coffin going into the church. I didn't think they'd go that far. I didn't do anything to provoke him to do what he done to me. After all that, week after week of this storm, I couldn't believe my ears, when 2 or 3 people who I didn't know very well, realised it was me who he indecently assaulted, said he'd done all this before, and it was kept quiet by the victim because she did get a house.

The church, which that coffin went into, had side buildings, which India used to go to the playgroup there. One of the assistants, came up to me as I was paying, saying rubbish like "Hmm, could there have been a mistake, or misunderstanding?" I said "What?" She said "Surely he wouldn't do anything like that". She then put her arms up towards my arms to clasp her hands on them, saying "Surely he only did that", but I stepped back, saying to her "Will you get off me! Was you actually there!? No! You wasn't!" I know what he done to me ok!"… and off we went, with me ad libbing about 'Not staying around here where they support perverts'. . Oh dear, those poor people in their own little world, putting it to rights and preaching to others every day, whilst protecting the perverts.

LAST THOUGHTS

This whole read is true...Well you wouldn't want to make that lot up anyway.

I've sought no help towards this book, apart from the legal stuff, and confirmation checks on 'Dictionary'.

Millions of words have been streaming through my head, but many of those words left me unconfident to use them until I checked their proper meaning. Well, what else can be expected from a 57year old woman with a patchy, sabotaged education, and all those years ago? It was never going to be an intellectual read... There's been no reason for needing any other kind of help because it's out of others' hands.

Words have been pouring out, full of dads' dirt, and all the crap that's emanated from it. It was a matter of un-jangling it all to a chronological order and I now hope, with clarity.

Nearly every day, my head loads up and feels like Operation Stack, pressuring me to write, before I turn into an explosion of anger and revenge.

The main title, I feel completely surrounds my life.

"Adult Child" for obvious reasons of doing adult acts throughout my childhood.

"Childish Adult" frankly, sums me right up. My nature is said to be bubbly. I'm actually giggling my way out of trouble, from stuff I just don't get, in conversations. Debates on politics, discussions at work and social media often lose me, and this is when I dissociate and rejoin when I've understood something heard. It's that same dissociated state I sink into when guys tell me "You love it" after telling me my "breasts need massaging and tweaking, so, does that turn you on?" If I can answer before I'm swallowed into that state again, I reply with "My breasts have served their purpose for my baby. Why the hell would my own breasts turn me on!?". Then I'm blinded with flashbacks of the bath times, shoulders forward and dad groping me. Eventually, real-time comes back.

I can't grow up or act my age for love nor money, and not about to try now, sod it!

I laugh at things I really shouldn't laugh at. My education and trust was sabotaged before it got off the ground. I haven't a hope in hells' chance now. So yes, all summed up in one title.

The 'Darkly To Dad, And Back' title, in The Flats chapters stems from the many dark moments, like the bathroom light going off ready for dads' sex abuse to start. Then there was our bedroom sex, which was at night. There was the absolute, harrowing fear I had, from dad's' stories about the outside world at night. Then the smothered, shaded, claustrophobic feeling when dad was on top of me, during him raping me. All those dark moments, encompassed with the sinister nature of it.

The 'And Back' part is because of the similarities to 'Stockholm Syndrome', with me always looking up to dad as someone who I felt I owed and obeyed to since our sex and the deep secret.

With all dads' wrong doing, I was still toing and froing between ours' and Roses' flats, to see dad, like a return ticket for sex abuse. Then, when I became my own wild adult, I'd start ignoring him, and then somehow end up talking with him again, like nothing's been wrong between us.

This volatile relationship continued across the seventies, eighties, nineties and until twenty-twelve… but it isn't happening again.

What went on in dads' mind, to constantly commit almost the worst, life ruining crime upon a child, his own child at that?

Could it have been power over my age, strength and innocence? Or could it have been his small penis was made to feel bigger against my 5 year old vagina… and hands?

What made dad think he 'ruled' the occupants of our flat. 'Ruled', as opposed to nurtured. Broke the law horrifically, as opposed to protect and encourage.

This is the same subhuman who had the gall to stand in my house criticizing my beautiful, fun-loving India's' make up and clothing, after ogling her up and down. He's the same piece of dirt who, time after time in the sixties and seventies, lectured us three kids on manners, manners towards others, manners at the dining table and who, during all the years since clearing off with Mums' ex best friend, expressed his high and mighty words to me, on how he cleans around the home, and to look smart when outdoors, with the expectation of me following suit, all of which *he* only did since he started shagging Rose. Yes, shagging your wife's best friend! Where's your loyalty and respect huh!? But before Rose, he was rarely bothered about helping Mum. He was too busy tampering with cars and sniffing around the lone parent mothers, with his Tenants' Association as his cover. Oh, and sexually abusing me during certain time slots of no mum…He who's the same greb, who done a one off visit to my flat in Erith, (more like an inspection) then said, *"Well I'm pleased to see your home is clean love, I thought you'd be more like your mother. So why do you wear dirty looking jeans? People think you come from a dirty scruffy home when they see you out in tatty jeans all the time"*…

Oh dear… Always criticized Mum, when she couldn't be there to defend herself…How powerful did that make you feel?. My jeans, and "tatty jeans, all the time?"… The jeans, which I had several pairs of, and were all washed regularly, were part of my character as a motorcyclist. It would've looked a bit bloody stupid with some woollen mini skirt on like ya second wife lived in and lifted day in day out! You drivelling hypocrite you! I hardly saw dad once I was with my partner of the biking days.

This is the very same vile, hypocritical bigot, who lied to the Wiltshire CID and a Wiltshire Law Courts' Judge, and other members of the sad excuse of a family, who believed him. One of whom knows about the abuse first hand, 'knock, knock' on the bathroom door.

You're a deluded liar mate… criticizing Mum, me and India, like *we're* the dirty lowlifes. At least Mum dressed decently! She may've dragged us three non-angels up, but she done it without a penny or a helpful visit from you. She struggled all the way, but she done it without you… Now India, what the hell did she do wrong to be criticized and judged by you? Ah yes of course, she was young and female, just the type who you feel power over. Then me, having to put up with your lectures, criticisms and always judged by you…Yeah, *me* judged by *you* all my life.

How dare *you* judge others. It's not like you've been lawful, loyal and clean or honest yourself is it, having used your own child for sexual satisfaction.

You've actually been poison to my childhood and onto adulthood.

YOU, who **raped** your own six year old daughter, and spent years **sexually abusing** too. **YOU**, who ruined a marriage and family, and spent your parents' inheritance money on your new family and home, with **nothing for your own flesh and blood**, and **YOU** again, who **lied** to the Police, **lied** in the Law Courts, **lied** to your supporters.

And **YOU** turn around and tell people how ill-mannered and unclean *they* are!? Tut fuckin' tut…**Shame on YOU!**

There's definitely a pattern formed towards the denial of the prosecution of my dad here. The Crown Prosecution Service's found their own reasons, which go all round the houses, using snippets of irrelevant information to avoid the trial starting, and the so called witnesses' statements, which also took a wide berth from the truth. There was one proper witness, and he ducked out, by also going all round the houses to avoid the truth being spilled, by slating me about other subjects, and even when the witnesses were questioned about the inappropriate behaviour against me, they denied all knowledge of it. I don't raise hell from the age of six during many family rows, because I was brought up by a decent set of parents now do I. Where it all went wrong, was as I was growing up, well, trying to, but dad interrupted my growth and development, from which, you can tell by me writing this book, So there's no need for me to thank them for dashing in all directions from the truth, but glad to never have anything more to do with that small bunch of lying, dirty low-lives.

No one's a winner here.

- The trial was never reinstated, which could be seen as the CPS winning, but the trial only didn't go ahead because the CPS confused themselves over an alleged, allegation about some *second* rape, and then those 'irrelevant to the case', remarks I made, which *may* have undermined my case in court. So the cancelling of the trial wasn't based on believing there's no chance of a successful prosecution, or because of insufficient evidence. Why bring up twelve charges if they thought there was no chance of successful prosecution or not enough evidence?
- The cancelled trial did not mean dad is innocent, and neither can he *become* innocent once he used a minors' body… *my* child-body for sexual satisfaction. You can't turn the time back and erase your disgusting, vile acts upon me. You're always, always guilty.

- The twelve charges are still so… Nothing's been done about them, and those charges against dad, continue waiting to be judged or revenged upon. No one said the words 'charges dropped', to me and yes, they're still very much alive in my mind, and yours aren't they dad.

- Dad definitely hasn't won either. He'll believe he has won, because of no more court appearances, but this subhuman knows for real, deep down he's guilty. He tries to believe he's innocent, but give him a truth drug and you'd hear a repeat of my video statement and what I've written in this book… and who knows there could be more of his vile sex crimes done to me, that rests in my subconscious mind…

- I certainly didn't win. I can't turn the time back, and erase my abused childhood. I can't look forward with complete positivity yet because there's no telling when I'll be flashing back to the abuse etc etc… But, all that *has* resurfaced, is now down in black and white as the truth and nothing but.

Time to say a massive, heartfelt thanks to my stunning Daughter India.

Throughout her over disciplined, over protected and lone-parented childhood, it's me who's had the tantrums, from which India became her own adult child, having fast learned personal protection, respect and empathy at such a young age, and grown to become a fun-loving hard working and clever young adult.

India, whether you're a Paramedic or HGV driving Mumma yourself, whatever you do, I'm full of love and pride for you m'girly! X

Lightning Source UK Ltd.
Milton Keynes UK
UKHW041853290719
347034UK00003B/86/P